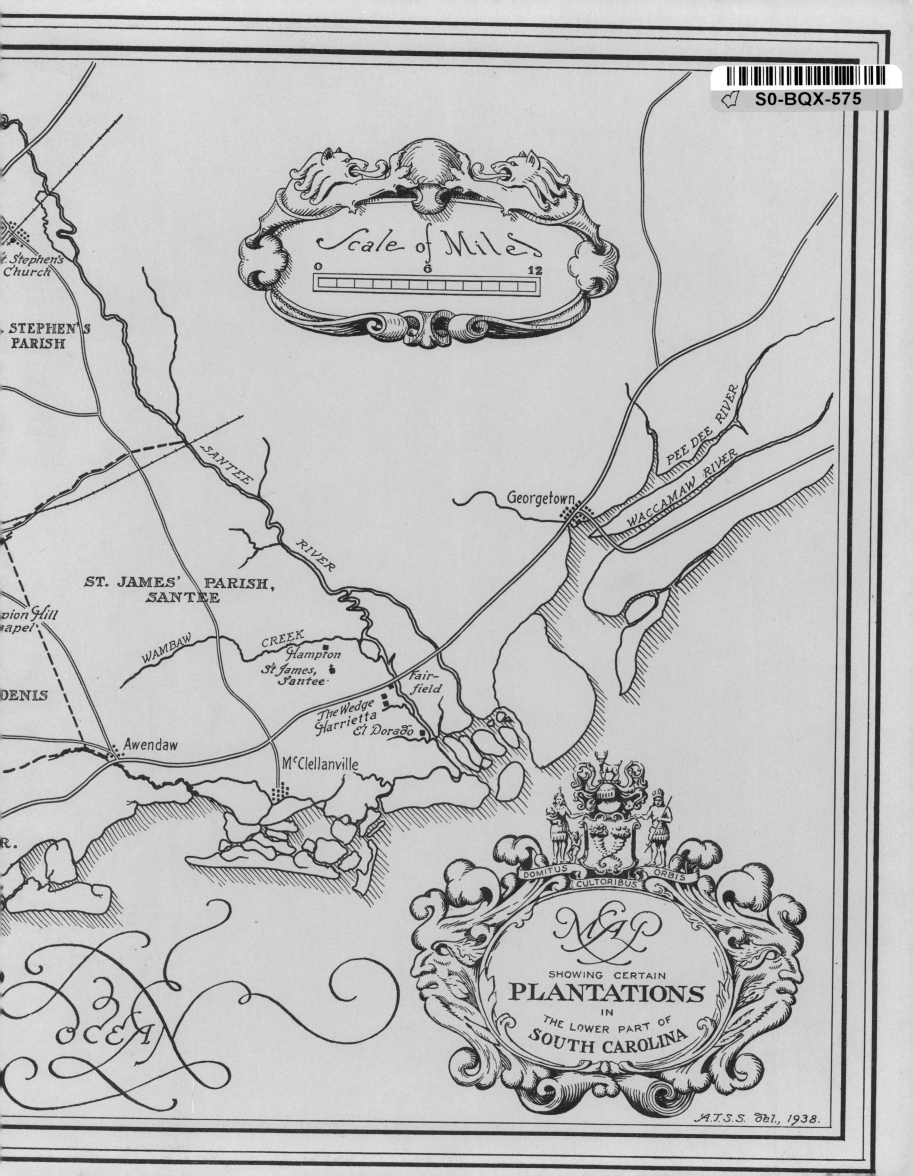

Scale of Miles

0   6   12

t. Stephen's
Church

ST. STEPHEN'S
PARISH

SANTEE

RIVER

PEE DEE RIVER

WACCAMAW RIVER

Georgetown

ST. JAMES' PARISH,
SANTEE

pion Hill
hapel

WAMBAW

CREEK

Hampton
St James,
Santee

Fairfield

DENIS

The Wedge
Harrietta
El Dorado

Awendaw

McClellanville

R.

OCEAN

DOMITUS   CULTORIBUS   ORBIS

MAP

SHOWING CERTAIN

PLANTATIONS

IN

THE LOWER PART OF

SOUTH CAROLINA

A.T.S.S. del., 1938.

PLANTATIONS
of the
CAROLINA LOW COUNTRY

PLANTATIONS
of the
CAROLINA LOW COUNTRY

By

SAMUEL GAILLARD STONEY

Edited by

ALBERT SIMONS, *F. A. I. A.*

&

SAMUEL LAPHAM, Jr., *F. A. I. A.*

With an Introduction by

JOHN MEAD HOWELLS, *F. A. I. A.*

PUBLISHED BY THE CAROLINA ART ASSOCIATION
CHARLESTON, SOUTH CAROLINA

To

FRANCES & WILLIAM EMERSON
who have wrought at home and abroad
to preserve for the future
the architectural heritage of the past

THE AUTHOR AND THE EDITORS ACKNOWLEDGE THEIR GRATEFUL APPRECIATION TO THE FAMILIES OF A GREAT MANY BUILDERS OF THESE HOUSES, FOR INFORMATION AND THE USE OF THEIR PAPERS AND MUNIMENTS: TO THE OWNERS OF THESE HOUSES FOR PERMISSION TO TAKE PHOTOGRAPHS: TO MISS ELLEN M. FITZSIMONS AND THE STAFF OF THE CHARLESTON LIBRARY SOCIETY FOR UNFAILING AID: TO LANGDON CHEVES FOR INFORMATION AND KIND ADVICE: TO THE LATE D. E. HUGER SMITH AND MISS ALICE R. HUGER SMITH FOR MUCH INFORMATION AND CRITICISM: TO H. R. SHURTLEFF FOR HIS GREAT ENCOURAGEMENT AND MOST HELPFUL CRITICISM: TO MISS MARIE H. HEYWARD AND J. WATIES WARING FOR INFORMATION: TO ROBERT N. S. WHITELAW, DIRECTOR, AND THE STAFF OF THE CAROLINA ART ASSOCIATION FOR PREPARING THEIR MATERIAL FOR PUBLICATION

CONTRIBUTIONS FROM THE AMERICAN COUNCIL OF LEARNED SOCIETIES TO MISS FRANCES B. JOHNSTON FOR ADDITIONAL PHOTOGRAPHS AND TO THE CAROLINA ART ASSOCIATION HAVE ASSISTED IN THE PUBLICATION OF THIS VOLUME.

NOVEMBER 1, 1938

INTRODUCTION TO THE
FIRST EDITION

THE historical and archeological interest of the remarkable group of buildings making up this book has been so ably and really seizingly presented by Mr. Samuel Gaillard Stoney in his text that to an outsider, and an architect, there can be left only the effort to evaluate the material of the book as architectural documents.

I place the value high. The group here shown is only what is left of a vastly larger group, destroyed by accident, war and earthquake.

These plates show American homes and must always be of value as architectural material for other American homes. They are so straightforward in their answer to climatic and social needs and to the limiting demands of building material that they give an answer to many of the same needs of today, for we like in our homes today just about the same kind of interiors, with open hearths and sunny windows, that our ancestors did, and much the same arrangements for entertaining our friends. We cannot copy exactly these old American homes for our new American homes, if only because we must change the kitchen services and add plumbing.

In trying for as much dignity and beauty as these houses achieved, we must be as frank in responding to our needs as they were. So I feel that the practising architect everywhere, but most in America, will find great value in these documents. The archeologist or purist in early American styles will find interest therein, but even the modernist will find pleasure in their straightforward creation of forms as they needed them and in the variations of elements, even to their columniations to suit their practical needs.

Many people have given their help in the making of this book. Proper credit is given, where possible, to those who have prepared the drawings. There is little need to comment on the contribution of the photography of Miss Frances Benjamin Johnston, with her flair for getting the best out of a dwelling, as well as the earlier photographic work of Mr. Ben Judah Lubschez. To Dr. and Mrs. William Emerson, grateful appreciation is due for their support, which has made this venture possible. There is another word of appreciation that I want to add, if only for my own satisfaction: and that is for the really remarkable maps and plan of Mr. Augustine Stoney. I had the privilege of seeing these in the original, and the more I studied them the more they revealed, as for instance, the garden plan of Middleton Place, whose history is so inviting.

With this volume, Messrs. Simons and Lapham have another well-accomplished have thus given to the other members of their profession, and in the recognition, by a task to their credit. I hope that they may find part of their reward in the help they much wider non-professional audience, of their presentation of these records of their native section.

JOHN MEAD HOWELLS, New York, June, 1938

HOW THE BOOK WAS MADE

It was inevitable; too many people in the Low Country saw that such a thing must be done. In 1928 many of these old houses were at such a low ebb of survival that a visual recording of them was needed at once.

That spring a generous spirit, William Emerson of Boston, put heart into the project by offering financial aid and the services of an expert photographer. The editors, who had already gained considerable knowledge of the houses in their practice, began plans for the book. In the winter Ben Judah Lubschez took a very full set of photographs and work was begun on a text.

Work was started also to get records the camera could not make. Time was snatched from busy lives to explore and measure for elevations and plans. Sunday after Sunday the parties went out. Sometimes it was lone men or a team of them. Sometimes there were grandly mixed parties of men, women and children. Everyone worked; the men with grandiloquent gestures of machetes clearing underbrush grown second story high, the women with soon toughened thumbs pressing the ends of tapes to crumbling walls, the children clearing trash and rubbish so that buried corners could be found and lost partitions located. Thus we covered houses and churches in fair order, and buildings only piles of earthquake rubble, gardens in full glory, and gardens hidden under scrub pine and snaky briar patches; all were measured and their plans delineated. Probably the workers enjoyed the ruins most, because each could speculate gloriously on the details that were hopelessly lost.

Then when the book was ready for publication the depression stopped everything. For years the project remained a determination in the minds of the collaborators. At last in 1938, ten years after its beginning, ways were found. The Carolina Art Association, having long seen the value of this work, came forward as publishers. The American Council of Learned Societies made grants for costs of printing and for Frances Benjamin Johnston to take photographs that would complete the record. In the light of fresh studies the text was completely rewritten. Most able and sympathetic printers were obtained, the book came out at last and to a very pleasant success.

HARRIET PORCHER SIMONS

THE COUNTRY AND THE PEOPLE

EVEN if you have no leaning towards the doctrine of predestination, the story of the Low Country can almost persuade you that this coastal region of South Carolina was foreordained to plantations. You will find that they have been there as long as white men have lived in the region. The lay of the land, its sorts, its climate, even the way its tidal rivers run, fitted it for them peculiarly. The men who settled it, the plans and ambitions that brought them and the successes that kept them there, and all the larger details of the history they and their successors made there, inclined the country to a spacious system. Even the staples the plantations throve by seem to have entered more or less consciously into this scheme, for when one failed another was soon found to replace it; for instance, when rice, the crop *par excellence* of the region, tired out one sort of land, other methods and vastly richer kinds of land were found for growing it. So well set was the system that it survived with some success the violent destruction of its natural era, and died so slowly that a few Low Country plantations persisted until these last decades, when a new ownership came into their old country, clearing its brush-grown fields, rebuilding the storm-riven rice field banks, refurbishing the old houses, and giving its plantations something more than a promise of a new lease on life.

Unfortunately there is nothing left of the Low Country's first plantations, for though they were few and at best temporary, they were made by the people who introduced the system in America, the Spanish. The coast of this part of its province of Florida was long one of Spain's imperial problems. From the time of old Ponce de Léon the country had been so unlucky to every Spaniard who went there that at last Philip II threw it bodily out of his dominion. At once he had to fight to take it in again, for promptly the French placed two successive Huguenot settlements on the coast, one at Charlesfort, on Port Royal in the Low Country, the next at Fort Caroline on the St. John's River in Florida proper. A vision of foreign flags flying on a coast that was a perfect network of harbors, inlets and islands, and within all too easy raiding distance of the Gulf Stream that runs along it, the homeward highway of the Spanish treasure fleets, gave the king other ideas of Florida. So there was commissioned for the country an adelantado, one Menendez de Avilés, who, after summarily slaughtering the Huguenots, proceeded to protect his provinces by setting up the Presidio of San Augustin de la Florida and by trying to settle other military posts and support civilian communities to the northward. It was when these lesser posts failed and failed again that the ever-devoted mission brothers, Franciscans and Jesuits, were called in to charge themselves with another forlorn hope of the wide-flung empire. And the half-religious, half-military stations they made, remade and maintained along the Sea Islands were surrounded with villages of Indian converts and supporting plantations.

None, however, was lasting. Even St. Augustine, the head and heart of the system, was kept alive by steady transfusions of life from Hispaniola or Cuba. The supporting missions were constantly suffering from raids by the hostile Indians of the mainland or by freebooters from the sea. The converts revolted, or they and their pastors were wiped out by white men's diseases, so that the missions had frequently to be begun again. And at last the Carolinians made a clean sweep of them to within sight of the strong Castle of San Marco, which their coming had caused to be built beside St. Augustine.

Nearly the only certain relics of this life now to be found in the Low Country are the holy names, like that of St. Helena, left behind by the missions on their islands. The nearest thing to an architectural heritage the South Carolina plantations had of the Spanish is the system of building in concrete, called tabby. This was made of seashells in part burned to lime for the binder, in part more or less crushed for the aggregate, and cast between board forms much as is concrete today. It was used wherever there was an ample supply of shell, as along "the salt" where big kitchen-middens almost purely made of shell had been left by ancient coastal Indians. Where shell could be got forts, breakwaters, churches, entire plantation establishments, even to the roofs of smoke houses, were cast solid of tabby. Its origin, its name and its tradition are all so distinctively of Spanish derivation that any unidentified bit of it found in the Low Country is usually set down as their handiwork, until disappointingly demonstrated to be of far later date.

The great plantation age of the Low Country began with the conception of the idea of Carolina in the mind of a Barbadian planter, as a land for planters and plantations. Its actual commencement dates from the birth of the colony by the aid of an English country gentleman, a certain Sir John Colleton, who just after the Restoration brought the idea to London. He was an old cavalier who had spent a fortune of £40,000 for the King, raised and fought a regiment at home in England and, after defeat there, had fled to Barbadoes, been defeated again and at last turned planter on the island. Since that time Colleton had seen the spread of the sugar plantations, with their slave-grown crop, absorbing steadily the smaller land-holdings by which the island had been settled. As steadily, a stream of people was squeezed out to the other British colonies—dispossessed men, the ambitious and land-hungry, bondsmen who had served their time and could find no land fit to set up on, people of all sorts salted to colonial life and trained in plantation ways; this stream it was Colleton's plan to divert to the semi-tropic debatable land that lay vacant, or half-heartedly held by the Spanish, along the great curve of coast between Virginia and St. Augustine.

In London Colleton associated to his scheme seven others who deserved much from King Charles. Of these, Hyde, Earl of Clarendon; the Earl of Craven; Lord Berkeley; Sir William Berkeley, the Cavalier Governor of Virginia; and Sir George Carteret, the Cavalier founder of New Jersey; had like Colleton made many sacrifices for the royal cause; while George Monk, Duke of Albemarle, and Anthony Ashley-Cooper, then Lord Ashley, had accomplished more towards the Restoration than the others put together by their eleventh-hour shift from the Commonwealth. The most of this company were already involved in a number of great colonial and trading promotions that were then spreading the British empire to all quarters of the globe. As a basis for a new venture Charles II readily granted them a vast and vastly unknown part of North America. This was simply included between the coasts of the Atlantic and the South Sea, and bounded north and south by a pair of parallels of latitude. One of these parallels has remained in part as the south line of Virginia; the other, for many reasons never surveyed, was to have begun at a point on the coast some sixty-odd miles south of St. Augustine. In the King's honor a name that had hung on loosely to this part of Florida ever since the subjects of Charles IX of France had tried to take it was revamped into Carolina, and the Province was ordered to be settled and ruled by its grantees, as Lords Proprietors.

Colleton, through his associates in Barbadoes, at first tried to settle West Indians in Carolina on the Cape Fear River. His colony, after serving as a base for surveys and explorations of the coast to the southward, broke up and ended, and it was not until Sir John's death threw the control of Carolina into the most able hands of Lord Ashley that the scheme began to work.

From this sickly little man, almost a genius, the Low Country got a running start towards plantations, and a good deal besides. He had been, or was to be, a soldier, a statesman, a politician, something of a Restoration rake-hell (though he had to live with a golden tube let into his liver), a judge of ability, a patriot of discernment, an amateur philosopher and a shrewd promoter. But at bottom he was an hereditary landlord, firmly attached to his old semi-feudal manors in Dorsetshire.

His problem in settling Carolina was dual: to capture the Indian trade of the vast territory for his syndicate and to settle the land as quickly and as solidly as possible with future tax-payers. He drew upon his various experiences of life to help in the task. With the aid of John Locke, the celebrated philosopher, his secretary and his lifelong friend, Ashley planned the colony and concocted a Fundamental Constitution for its governance, larding the latter liberally with propaganda and bait for the sorts of peoples then on the move whom he hoped to steer towards Carolina.

At bottom this Fundamental Constitution was a grand compromise between extreme freedom in belief and an almost feudal safeguarding of property. Land, the great inducement, was to be given to all comers who acknowledged themselves at least Deists. Even slaves were to have allotments that went to their masters, a proviso especially cooked up for the taste of the West Indians. To the Protestants of Europe, then harried with the persecutions of the Counter Reformation, a novel refuge was offered where, if a man but acknowledged that there was a God and that He was publicly to be worshipped, the methods and manners of so doing were left to his own taste, and where seven people likeminded in such matters might set up their own church. And as an attraction to young Englishmen of pith, full of the heraldic glamor of the Restoration, and to all men of ambition or substance, there were provided two titles of hereditary nobility, Landgrave and Cacique. The nobles were to be picked by the Proprietors from the worthies of their Province as it grew, to help them govern and stabilize it, and they and their great land grants of baronies were to be so scattered through the colony as to "avoid the erection of a numerous democracy."

Being the work of philosophers the Constitution had touches of the purely Utopian. It forbade the practice of law for money. As was natural to the time when it was written, it contained bits of real feudalism, as in the allowance to any landowner of fair estate of the right to have his property set up into a manor, though cannily enough, he was left to catch for himself the leet-men, who as hereditary bondsmen were to tenant it.

Meantime, most practically, Ashley started colonists towards Carolina. He made the Proprietors go into their pockets liberally to support the affair. He himself advised and regulated for it wisely and ably, for he ordered the beginning of the first Low Country plantation with the commencement of the settlement, both to help feed the settlers and to experiment in such money crops as it was hoped might thrive there. Later, when plans were being made for the town that grew into Charleston, he tried to insure that fair-sized streets, regularly laid out, would be provided for it, and room kept for its future decent growth. At last, when he had come into disgrace from his opposition to the King, he petitioned vainly that he be allowed to retire to his estates in Carolina, where, from his barony of St. Giles on Ashley River, he might personally help with the building of the colony.

His Constitution had more effect on the colony as propaganda than as a real basis of government, but certain of its provisions seem to have continued their work long afterwards and by indirection. No Low Countryman ever asked for manorial privileges, but the self-contained plantations soon had most of the stability Ashley had hoped to get with the old form. His titled nobility was never held in peculiar respect in the colony, and their unwieldy baronies were most of them soon cut up into plantations. But the planter people who bedevilled the Landgraves and Caciques out of existence never quite forgot them, and long afterwards, in the days of the Romantic Revival, planters with more wealth and influence than the Carolina nobility could have boasted, looked back with a touch of longing at the lost pageantry of their names and the ordered labelling of their powers.

Ashley's provisions for the things of the spirit more readily survived. To their success as bait was partly due the highly individualistic society of the Low Country. But as well they served as something to be invoked, held on to, conjured with at least, while the colony was a yeasty mass of divergent peoples and politics, working to find itself.

Ashley's first contingent of settlers, being a mixture of people, was already characteristic of the future Low Country before they set sail from the Downs in the August of 1669. Aboard the three ships were English, Irish and Welsh, of all sorts too, but fairly proportioned with solid stock, younger sons of squires and well-taught men who could turn a phrase neatly in their letters, people who would take root and leave families that have prospered in the Low Country to this day. And before the expedition had finished an Odyssey, including two shipwrecks and a routing that took them by way of Ireland, Barbadoes, the Antilles in general, the Bahamas and Bermuda, the company it brought to Carolina had a further mixture with it of West Indians and at least three Negroes and was truly a proper beginning for the conglomerate Low Country.

It was true to Low Country ways too that the first act of this band, upon its arrival at its promised land, was to hold a disputed election, even before it had come ashore, and that its second should be to remove itself from the place to which it had been sent to one of its own choosing. This last performance was a piece of the purest good fortune. Port Royal, the harbor selected for the colony, was speciously spacious, indefensible, open to storms, and close to the surviving Spanish missions, while Charleston harbor, to which they went, was one of the finest on the coast of the Proprietors' grant, and naturally the heart of the rich region that was to become the Low Country. The change was made at the entreaty of a local Indian, the clever Chief of the Kiawahs. Several of the coast tribes had competed to get the whites as neighbors, allies to help them against a predatory people called the Westoes who had lately become the bullies of the region. Incidentally, this taking of sides in Indian quarrels at once became the basis of Carolina's Indian policy.

Four years before Charles-Town was begun on a very defensible little point west of the Kiawah's river, explorers prophetically named it the Ashley. And with the commencement of the town the first plantation was laid out by Ashley's orders, just to the south of the creek where the settlement had been made, where in that pioneer spring both cotton and indigo were planted in the Low Country.

Also in that first year land was set aside for a town on the peninsula called White Point, where very soon the future city of Charleston began its growth. And in that summer the Spanish initiated the little, private, intercolonial war that was to be kept up between St. Augustine and Charles-Town for a long lifetime. The first small armada St. Augustine sent up the coast in this opening year was, with its auxiliary force of Indian pettiaugers, caught in a hurricane, however, and blown out of all temper and condition for a fight, so that these new trespassers in Spanish domain were given time to establish themselves in peace.

At first the colony felt the need of experienced planters, but when it began to look sufficiently safe to tempt prudent men to it the need was more than supplied. The stream Colleton had tried to divert there was in such full flow towards Carolina in the first half-dozen years of the settlement at Charles-Town that the West Indians then became the most numerous part of the population. With their numbers, their experience and the working wealth they brought in the shape of slave gangs, they soon began to dominate the community. Crews of Negroes were increasingly brought in, for, due to the provision of land to them, their importation automatically gave their owners a plantation upon which to put them to work. So full was the early colony of West Indians that it was long classed almost as one of the Antilles that had drifted against the continent of North America.

The very process of making and stocking the first plantations strengthened this connection. The first exports from Charles-Town were puncheons for hogsheads and timber got in clearing lands and sent to the sugar islands to be traded for muscavado, which could be turned into hard money in England. Such new ground crops of the "bread kind" as corn and cow-pease were readily sold to Antillean planters too busy with their cane to make food. And since cattle and hogs were found to thrive phenomenally in the virgin pastures of the Low Country savannahs and swamps, salt meats were soon added to make a general provision trade, which long remained one of the chief minor industries of the plantations and a lasting link with their ancestral islands.

One of the marks of this intercourse is the Low Country's own peculiar Gullah. Early derived from peasant dialects of English bondsmen in the islands, mouthed into comfortable shape by the Negroes, the base of Gullah was a sort of plantation *lingua franca* developed in Barbadoes and Antigua, from whence it was brought to the Low Country to be further improved and varied on the rice plantations. Gullah is now a speech to itself, but it is still more closely related to that of the West Indians than it is to any other of the continental dialects.

From the beginning the spread of the plantations of the Low Country followed its rivers and creeks. The coast of South Carolina is well supplied with waterways. Three broad, if short, rivers drain into Charleston harbor, and out of it in both directions spread the tidal streams that cut the Sea Islands from the mainland. At the time of the settlement these streams, with hardly a haul-over, among them furnished a natural route whereby a pettiauger or canoe might pass from the mouth of the Santee, fifty miles above Charles-Town, to the mouth of the St. Mary's, about the same distance above St. Augustine, without risking the force of the open ocean except at a few spots along the way. The Indians knew the route well; the Spaniards' missionaries had improved and used it; the Carolinians were to spread their settlements along it, and from it up their rivers; and the Low Country was to continue to use it as a principal highway for heavy hauling as long as the old dispensation of plantations existed there.

Rivers and creeks were not only the safest routes of travel for the people of this dense-grown country, but they long remained the easiest and most comfortable to use. The Low Country is a land of alluvials whose soft loams, fine sands, heavy clays, deep swamp mucks and bottomless river marshes offer a variety of problems to a road builder. There is hardly any stone worth the mentioning in it, except certain outcroppings of marl, most of it too soft to be counted or used as stone. The trunks of the giant cypresses of the Low Country swamps furnished admirable material from which to dig out excellent canoes, and the people of the coast were long quite content to use their "dug-outs" as general vehicles, in their progresses from plantation to plantation or their journeys to town.

Ashley's plans for the settlement of Carolina had projected a number of semi-independent colonies. Each of these was to have a port-town whose supporting grants were to lie along rivers, after the fashion set by such northern colonies as Connecticut and, as there, every grant was to have one side on navigable water. But Low Country conditions vetoed the first part of this program, for most of the rivers were too shallow for ocean-going shipping, and by the time that the three streams which flowed into Charles-Town harbor were settled out in plantations, that town had established itself as the port of the Low Country, as well as its capital, its mother city and the logical center of its life. The plantations themselves served both to build up the city and break down any rivals that sprang up about it. Towns continued to be projected; a few of them even got off the parchments where they had been mapped and on to solid ground; but the plantations were all the while becoming more self-sufficient, virtually each of them a village in itself that took its trade, as it carried its produce, to Charles-Town. So, if there were cross-road stores in the Low Country, Charles-Town, except for Beaufort and George-Town and in spite of them, remained the place where you bought and sold seriously. To this day if a Low Countryman says "town," he means Charleston.

In the first decade of the colony mixed lots of emigrants from England and groups of West Indians had continued to come into it. In 1680 the population advanced with a bound, with the gain of two new sorts of settlers brought to South Carolina partly by Ashley's promises of religious liberty. These were the Huguenots and the English Dissenters.

The Huguenots were induced by Crown agents working in France to go to Carolina where, it was hoped, they could make the wine, the oil and the silk for which England sent so much gold across the Channel. These people, flying before the wrath that was to come when Louis XIV revoked the Edict of Nantes, blazed a path for a number of their co-religionists who continued to come to the colony until the end of the century. They were the first and by far the most vigorous and potent of any of the groups of continental people to come into the Low Country. A few brought money or goods with them, but the most, and nearly all those who came after 1685, possessed little more than their courage and persistence. Yet in their second and third generations they were already taking rank with the first families of the community and making, with the English, marriages from which sprang many of the ablest and most brilliant Low Countrymen.

In the same year with this first Huguenot influx there came another lot of Calvinists, English Dissenters discontented under a monarchy, fearful of the time soon to come when the Catholic Duke of York would be king. So many of them arrived at this time that they outnumbered all the other elements of the population and for a while were able to spread a fair amount of puritanical confusion.

Chinked in between these major groups were smaller ones. These included Long Islanders who had left New Amsterdam for Carolina when their old colony was traded to the English for Surinam and Dutchmen straight from Holland whose leader, one Van Arrsens, left what has now become the oldest house in the Low Country. A colony of Scotch Covenanters sought to set up for themselves on Port Royal, but a few years afterwards, weakened by fevers and the jealousy of Charles-Town, their settlement of Stuartstown was snuffed out by a Spanish raid, although survivors remained in the Low Country to add to its mixture of peoples. Antipaedo-baptists tired of being persecuted for their beliefs by the authorities of Massachusetts came from Maine and took up land in what is now the neighborhood of Pinopolis, where Somerset and Somerton plantations still carry names they left. In 1696 a congregation from Dorchester in Massachusetts moved in a body to a Dorchester they made on the headwaters of the Ashley. Also in Charles-Town before 1700 were Sephardic Jews, Quakers and Irish Catholics.

Among these eminently respectable strains there also seeped in wild romantic bloods from the sea. Charles-Town was early a market for naval stores as well as for food stuffs, a thriving, pushing, not too orderly port where strange customers were not very closely questioned about the sources of the curious coins with which they wished to buy or of the odd lots of valuables they sought to barter. Armed ships were handy to have around in case the Spanish came up the coast, and if the King's customs officers from the northern provinces, or the Proprietors at home in London, scolded, it was after all a time when the difference between a privateer and a pirate depended on so many things that it was hard to draw a line unless you yourself happened to suffer from their work. And it was not until Charles-Town suffered that she discriminated.

Meantime, in 1692, one famous company of questionable seafarers anchored the ship *Loyal Jamaica* in Rebellion Roads, off Mount Pleasant, where it lay, giving Charles-Town some uneasiness. When peremptorily ordered away it put out to sea.

but added to the unrest by tacking back and forth across the harbor mouth before it finally disappeared. Shortly thereafter the authorities had word that the ship was run ashore in Sewee Bay, had been stripped of her furniture, and that her people were scattered into the town and country. Upon examination of some of them it proved that they had committed nothing like piracy, except in the Red Sea where the subjects of the Grand Mogul were then considered fair prey to Christians; that they had acted as privateers in the Caribbean, but that a debate begun upon their sailing north into the latitude of Charles-Town as to whether or not they should put in there and turn planter had been prolonged until they settled it in the affirmative by beaching their ship at Sewee. Several of these Red Sea men were well connected in England, young, and rich with the plunder of the paynims. Following the resolution they had taken, they became not only planters of Carolina but the ancestors, in some cases, of most eminent Low Country families.

Before any way of life could be worked out by such a mixture of peoples there were bound to be stresses and strains, even with a strong government and in a quiet land. But in Carolina after Ashley's day the Proprietors' rule weakened and then began to grow contemptible. The Province never paid the profits expected and proprietorial shares went on sale in London and were picked up by adventurous stock-brokers and Quakers. Even the Carolina titles, it was said in the Province, could be got, around 1700, for the payment of £100 for a landgraveship and half that sum for the honors of a cacique. So to injury was added insult.

Strong government, too, was greatly needed, for the Province was ringed in by the sea, the savages and the Spaniards, with all help afar off. In those days North Carolina asked but did not give aid, and there were many days' sailing between Charles-Town and Virginia, with the stormy headlands of Capes Fear, Lookout and Hatteras on the way.

So the cooped-up Low Country soon learned to take the initiative in its politics. The first group to do it effectively were the planters, a community of West Indians, mostly Barbadians, who had settled themselves together on Goose Creek, about sixteen miles from Charles-Town. Experienced and independent, part of the largest party in the Province before the coming of the Dissenters, these "Goose Creek Men" made themselves the bugbears of the Proprietors and their agents and governors.

When the Dissenters came to South Carolina the Proprietors deliberately pitted them against the Goose Creek Men, a course all the more easy because the latter were Churchmen, with Cavalier backgrounds. In the row that ensued the Dissenters had, besides their numbers, a contingent hold on the governorship because two of their leaders had been created Landgraves for bringing them out and others of them later got the title, and under the Constitution the senior Landgrave in the Province was a natural successor or appointee to a vacant governorship. By proper application of these factors their party virtually governed the Province for the last twenty years of the seventeenth century.

By so doing they drove into alliance all the other parties. The combination was led by the Goose Creek Men but the fight met on the devoted heads of the Huguenots, who while it lasted were gerrymandered out of their representation in the Assembly, then deprived of their votes, and last, as aliens, threatened with having their marriages treated as irregular, their children as bastards, and their properties as forfeit.

The struggle ended at last in a grand Low Country election in which the allies, having gained a single seat above their enemies, proceeded to make the Low Country safe from anything resembling a theocracy.

One of the first fruits of this victory was the establishment of the Church of England in South Carolina in 1706, the division of the Low Country into parishes and the erection of the first of the parish churches and chapels of ease that so long served the plantation people. But the most lasting result of the affair was the end of religious persecution in the rising Province, for thenceforth under the liberal sway of the planters, church and meeting-house were made to keep their place, and the Low Country as it flourished was able to build up its own peculiar culture uninhibited alike by "infidelity and enthusiasm."

While this matter was coming to a solution the Province found itself part of a triangle of exterior forces. Pushing their Indian alliances, the Carolinians had driven the Spanish out of all north and west Florida and saw their way to take over all the trade with the Indians of that part of the Proprietors' grant which lay to the east of the Mississippi; they were even laying plans to find and get hold of the mouth of that river when the French set down their colony of Louisiana there. The French proved harder customers to deal with than the Spanish had been. Thenceforth there were two frontiers to fight upon—one to the south, the other to the west—until the Bourbons took Spain and made them virtually one. However, on the outbreak of Queen Anne's War the new walls of Charles-Town successfully overawed a combined French and Spanish fleet.

For all the fighting with these new and old enemies the Indian trade continued to flourish. The Proprietors had tried to monopolize this business, but the pioneer planters broke into it and it was soon on its way to make Charles-Town second only to Albany as an Indian Trade town. Southern peltries were never so valuable as those got from the northern woods, but the territory west of Carolina furnished deer skins by tens of thousands. The trade in them equalled that of rice in value until the middle of the eighteenth century and the general business it gave to Charles-Town was separate from and independent of the Low Country.

Some of the by-products of the Indian trade vitally affected the plantations, even after they had ceased to be trading posts, for here as in other places the British Empire was spread at the expense of the aborigines. The Indians friendly to the South

Carolinians were kept at war with those allied to the Spanish or the French and when South Carolinians moved against either Florida or Louisiana their expeditionary forces had usually a proportion of ten Indians to one white man. The Indians paid for these troop movements mostly with their own red skins; for though Ashley had strictly forbidden that they be enslaved, his law was invoked apparently only as ammunition in political mud-slingings. Otherwise it was disregarded, and the colonies' soldiery even paid for active service with such captured Indians as could be saved from the tomahawks of their allies.

Of the enslaved Indians the braves, who were not particularly good workers and ready to run away as long as they were within a few hundred miles of their homes, were sold away—some to the north, chiefly in Massachusetts, the rest south to the sugar islands. The squaws, more biddable and complacent, and cheaper than Negro women, were used to balance the sexes in the plantation cabins and supply wives for Negro men. The resultant Mestees, or Mestizos, taking staunchness from their mothers and gentleness from their fathers, were the forerunners of the intra-plantation slave aristocracy—house and body servants, drivers and mechanics—and today you can still find Negroes in the Low Country boastful of their Indian descent.

The plantations themselves grew more or less directly at the expense of the Indians. Those who lived in the Low Country were as much dependent on fishing as on hunting or planting and had long since preëmpted what the whites found to be the best sites for plantation settlements. The needs were the same: a marsh-free landing on water deep enough to carry a canoe, a well-drained spot to live on, a spring of water, some high planting land. The Indians seem to have shared even the Low Country predilection for live oaks and encouraged if they did not plant them, relishing their shade and using their acorns for food. The patriarch of the grove of oaks found about most plantation houses had sometimes a history that goes back to Indian days. In the early scramble for land a great many small plantations, afterwards absorbed into large ones, put their houses where best they might, but arrow points and potshards found around the sites of all the finer houses are distinctive evidence that red men lived thereabouts before the coming of the whites.

At the beginning, working on the theory that the King's gift gave them a clear title, the Proprietors forbade any payment for land to be made to its Indian incumbents. Later, by Ashley's order, this was changed, but the strings of worthless beads, the yards of red cloth, the hatchets and sundries given for land made this arrangement largely a change from "force to fraud." This combination of things, fomented constantly by the continuing encroachment of planter whites upon the lands of hunting Indians, bred at last a grand outbreak.

What hastened most the spread of the plantations—the thing that changed many of them from units of land to the form they were to keep thenceforth in the Low Country—was rice. In 1663, soon after he had become a Proprietor of Carolina, the

Duke of Albemarle conjectured it would thrive there. Early explorers predicted its suitability to the "meadows" and "savannahs" they found along the coast. In 1672 the Proprietors sent out a barrel of rice to Charles-Town just in time for its spring planting. By the next year enough of a surplus was made to export a little. Later, probably in the early nineties, John Thurber, a New England ships-captain, brought in some seed from Madagascar. In 1715 he was duly rewarded, as the new strain seems to have increased both the quantity and quality of the crop. Certainly a bumper yield in 1696 embarrassed Charlestonians, first to get ships to carry it off, then to get it past the pirates its abundance had attracted. The indignation aroused by their behavior seems to have done more to turn the sentiment of the town against the gentry of "the grand account" than all the preachments of the Proprietors or the scoldings of the customs officers. Rice and respectability may be said thus to have come hand in hand into the Low Country and to have dwelled together there as long as plantations prevailed.

Rice was the money crop—virtually the money of the Province—for the Assembly allowed quit rents to be paid in it, and for over two hundred years its characteristics and requirements molded Low Country life as did nothing else. It was also a political crop, for in provincial times it started the deep-rooted Low Country belief in free trade, as the Province was soon able to oversupply the English market and steadily pushed to be allowed to sell it directly to the southern European countries where it was so popular. It fastened plantations firmly to the rivers, at first because its weighty tierces would have played hob with any Low Country road and later for the sake of the tidal rice fields made out of river swamps and marshes. It was even responsible for the Low Country's taste in Madeira, because much of the choicest wine of the rice-eating island came back to Charles-Town in trade.

The first Low Country rice fields were made in the savannahs that had been marked down for them by the explorers. There the crop seems to have been grown without much more than the natural dampness of the soil, much as it is now planted by the country Negroes. If its fields were banked at all, the small earthworks did little more than catch rainwater and resembled the great riverbanks of later days as the five-toed horse resembles a Shire stallion. Then, as men found that the thirsty plant rewarded them almost directly in proportion to the drink it was given, rice was moved into the inland swamps, the low-lying lands out of which the Low Country streams seep rather than run. These swamps were cut into sections with more sizable banks and the top, or head, division was kept flooded for a "reserve" of water with which to irrigate the lower ones that were used for fields. The swamps were at first the richest lands used in the country, the fields grubbed out of them were the prime necessity of a considerable plantation, and there is no early plantation house of any great dignity that does not stand near a big swamp of this sort. If today these swamps, long since depleted of their richness and abandoned, are so many tangles of jungle vegetation, there is none of them in the Low Country that cannot boast its old banks and ditches and even sometimes its old settlements, marked now only by heaps of mouldering bricks.

What the earliest plantation houses were like it is now hard to conjecture. When in 1732 a party of Scotch-Irish came into Williamsburg District, they found prepared for them houses of earth which from the story of the Witherspoon family appear to have been some sort of erection of poles, brush and sod. In 1682 Thomas Newe saw in Charles-Town (two years since transplanted to White Point) about a hundred houses "wholly built of wood, though there is excellent Brick made, but little of it." (How exactly his "wholly" may be interpreted is shown by old laws forbidding in the town chimneys contrived of other stuff than brick.) And even today we have the ubiquitous log-cabin of the Low Country, with chimneys made of sticks set up pig-pen fashion and daubed over (pargetted) liberally with straw-bound clay, and with foundations, or house blocks, of live oak or light wood in lieu of brick. There is also little or no sign of brick on the point of Old Town plantation where the first Charles-Town was built.

So far as existing houses are concerned, we come with almost a jump to the Medway house of the Dutchman Van Arrsens and find it, in a colony only sixteen years old, a fairly capacious dwelling with some pretense to esthetics in style and more than a pretense to esthetics in its pleasant situation. Van Arrsens' brick is notoriously bad, but so then were the brick Sir Christopher Wren had to use in his work and, according to Macauley, all that were made in England in those times. There is plenty of evidence that Van Arrsens was not alone in burning home-made brick for his house at that period and that experiments were being made with other materials. In 1700 John Lawson, on his way to North Carolina, stopped on French Santee with Joachim Gaillard, who was living in a "curiously contrived house built of brick and stone that is gotten near that place." The stone was a marl that outcrops along the Santee; just next to the Gaillard settlements it forms a bluff where the Huguenots had their church and laid out their never-built Jamestown, doubtless to avail themselves of one of the nearest approaches to a free-stone that can be found in the Low Country, and a material that would partially satisfy their Gallic taste for solid, lasting constructions. Marl was used elsewhere. On Wadboo Creek, at the head of the Cooper River's Western Branch, one of the Colletons quarried so fine a sort to build his barony house that Tuomey the geologist, when he first saw its ruins, mistook its walls and carved mantels for Portland stone.

When the Swedish fashion of building log houses came into the Low Country is not now known, but Ramsay reports that during the Yemassee War of 1715 a man in St. John's, Berkeley, had such a stout house of logs and such a collection of fierce dogs, trained to kill and eat Indians, that he was able to last out the trouble at home, when all his neighbors were flying to Charles-Town for safety.

From Van Arrsens' house, Medway, to Middleburg, the house of Benjamin Simons, the oldest of wood now standing in the Low Country, is another jump of years and development, for here is no longer a European dwelling set up in the middle of an American wilderness, but one that in its shape, its planning and its materials already shows a considerable understanding of the needs of the climate. The further leap to the very much developed house at Mulberry marks very vividly how in a half-century the Low Country had "arrived."

The architectural gap before these houses, the missing links between them, are partly accounted for by the first destructive war that came into the Low Country. When the Carolinians had devastated Florida they brought back and planted on their southern border, between the Edisto and the Savannah, a tribe of Indians called the Yemassees, whom they planned to keep as a buffer between them and the Spaniards. As time went on these people were so abused by ill-regulated trading and so irritated by the encroachment of settlers that in 1715 they broke out into a war which took the Province by surprise; they destroyed or looted some two hundred houses throughout the Low Country, driving even the prosperous Goose Creek people away from their plantations. It was a good while before the Province recovered from this trouble, but one long-desired improvement resulted—the change from proprietorial control to that of the Crown, in 1719.

The transition to Royal Government also made South Carolina a unit to itself, divorcing it from its last nebulous connections with North Carolina. And when in the 1730's colonies of Germans, of Swiss and of Scotch-Irish pushed the frontier away from the old parishes and the settlement of Georgia carried it well down the coast towards Florida, the Low Country was fairly established.

Partly it was these changes, partly the general prosperity of the British Empire, that caused the building in the Low Country, between 1720 and 1740, of such a number of houses which have survived to our time because of their solidity, their usefulness or their ornateness. In a way—certainly in the matter of plantation house building—it was the Augustan Age of the Low Country, for there such houses as Fenwick Hall, Drayton Hall and Crowfield were never again quite equalled, and Crowfield's garden was to be excelled but once in the elaborateness of its formal arrangement. Here also the architectural history of the plantations supplements that of the town, for with all the risks of fire in the country, the wholesale burnings of Charles-Town were more disastrously complete and left little of the building there from before 1750 to come down to us.

At that time also the town and the Low Country were taking on more noticeably the peculiar pattern of their interdependent life. The primacy of the town, set by its geographical position and its history, insured by the separate business of the Indian trade, was further developed by the steady interchange of life as well as business between it and the plantations. Thus its preëminence became and continued to be more a matter of concentration than of differentiation. People and families shuttling from town to plantation, living between them, and holding interest in both, wove a pattern of life like that of a Greek Colony or an Italian City-State, where the name of the city and its territory were interchangeable and where countrymen considered themselves to be, and were, almost equally the citizens of the town with those who dwelt in its streets.

Later, under the Republic, certain social barriers were set up from time to time between planting and the professions, and "trade," but under the Royal Government no such invisible line was drawn. Land and plantations were excellent investments for a business man's surplus or for the savings of a professional man or politician; a planter's life was a pleasant goal for their old age and an agreeable career for their children. So most prosperous town men were considerable planters as well. The patriarchal program by which planter families tried to set up their numerous sons each on his own place was limited, however, by the sizes of the no less patriarchal families then fashionable, and younger sons had to be sent to town to shuffle for themselves in the merchants' counting houses along the Bay.

Marriages between all the sorts of people in the Low Country—West Indians, Huguenots, Dissenters—went further to accomplish its amalgam, though in certain localities, as in Middle St. John's, Berkeley, with the Huguenots, more by the accident of environment than any deliberate choice, some strains of blood were kept unmixed. On the other hand, an aristocracy of birth was being distinctly formed among the families who had arrived at political or commercial prominence and wealth; the leaders in this aristocracy were the West Indians, the Goose Creek Men of the Proprietors' day, marrying their daughters and sons among each other and to the more fortunate of the other sorts of peoples.

Marriages also form a nice index of the rise of the Low Country in imperial estimation, for at this time South Carolina planters' daughters were first considered good matches for young sons of the English nobility, one of whom, by reason of a couple of lucky deaths, could give John Fenwick, of Fenwick Hall, the felicity of speaking of his daughter as the Countess of Deloraine.

The Established Church had too a stabilizing and a unifying effect on the Low Country people, for the second generation were willing to relinquish the convictions of their elders. So it was with the Huguenots, who at first, in spite of their political alliance with the Churchmen and also in spite of the liberal allowances made to them when they allied their congregations to the Establishment, yet found the act of kneeling to receive the sacrament and the crossing of their children in baptism a little too close to the Roman ritual for comfort, but who in the next generation sat freely on vestries and helped to build most of the parish churches in the Low Country.

The convenience of the parish churches and chapels, the fact that the Province helped to build them and supported them in part, and the equally important fact that they, their vestries and their ministers were part of the body politic, made it easier for plantation people to join their congregations. Then too, the Church of England, through the Society for the Propagation of the Gospel, kept the Province constantly supplied with ministers and helped, if necessary, to support them in their parishes; some of these missionaries were fantastically unfit for spiritual work, but most of them were worthy enough. Dissent in the plantation country flourished in spots, but the trend of the people towards Episcopalianism, however gradual the step might be, was fairly inevitable; on Edisto a Baptist congregation succumbed gradually to Presbyterianism but later the Episcopal Church was to take about a half of the people of the Island. In the middle of the eighteenth century, when bitterly plagued by the bumptiousness of George Whitfield, the Bishop of London's Commissary in South Carolina complained that the Church was there crucified between two thieves, Infidelity and Enthusiasm. But if his church had at the time some right to be fearful of the latter, the former had helped rather than hindered it in becoming the most considerable religious body of the Low Country.

The method of absorption of a Huguenot congregation into the Establishment is still witnessed by the name of one of the old parishes. When the people of French, or Orange, Quarter, one of the oldest Huguenot communities, decided to go over to the Anglican Church, their *pasteur* was ordained to English orders, they were supplied with a French version of the liturgy, and they were made into a parish within a parish. The first name of the section had been St. Thomas and now, in compliment to the patron saint of France, St. Denis was added, but the latter functioned within the former as a separate unit until towards the middle of the eighteenth century, when the French-speaking members of its congregation had almost entirely disappeared.

On the other hand, in Charleston the variety of old congregations, of old religious buildings or of their sites still go to show how long-lived Ashley's work for freedom of conscience was to be in South Carolina and how staunchly men kept to their opinions where there was any opportunity or encouragement to do so. That we have illustrated but one Presbyterian Church is in good part due to the modesty of that sect, who built their meeting houses of wood and with such plainness in the early days that men were insufficiently impressed by them to preserve them.

That the architecture of a country is not only the best illustration of its history but a fairly delicate indication of its status at various times is rather amusingly shown by the dates of the buildings covered by this book. The record they make is of necessity incomplete and scrappy, for all told, the Low Country has had three wars that took fair toll of its buildings; after the last of these the sudden shock to and long slow death of the plantation system carried off many a house through mere dilapidation, and in this life-time of destruction an earthquake that in its day was world news hastened the action of a semi-tropic climate and helped on the work of the fires that are the winter bane of the Low Country's pine forests. The simple fact that the post-bellum reduction of servants brought kitchens out of separate buildings that were provided almost for the purpose of being burned conveniently by Negro cooks and into the main plantation houses accounted for the loss of a fair percentage of them. Also, our recording has been kept by sundry circumstances to the oldest and richest part, architecturally speaking, of the Low Country and so is not entirely representative. Even so, the dates of the buildings covered by this book in chronological arrangement will form for you a neat indication of the economic ups and downs of the region. Thus the gap between the period of St. Andrew's, Goose Creek and Mulberry, and the buildings of the 1720's, shows the time taken up by the Yemassee War and the revolt against the Proprietors' government, and the necessary period of recovery. There is such a break between the construction of Drayton Hall (1738) and the building that began in 1753 with sudden fervor and ran on to the Revolution, a period that marks for us a decisive war between England, France and Spain which brought to the Low Country an agricultural crisis and from it a new crop. There is another long break between the dates of Lewisfield (1774) and the portico of Hampton (1791) as evidence of the effect of the Revolution, and a lesser disturbance of the stream of building occurs for the war of 1812.

Physically the Low Country was not touched by the French and Indian War, as Georgia was well enough established to take up the attacks from St. Augustine, but economically it suffered from the hurt to the rice crop through the sea-fighting and the disturbance of the south European markets. Planters searched for substitute staples and soon found one that became a most valuable addition to Low Country agriculture.

Cotton and indigo planted in the first year of the colony had survived as occasional crops. Some cotton had even been exported, but because of the onerous task of clearing it from its seed its production was too difficult for a country where cruder, less exacting work gave good returns on plantation capital, and cotton's day was not yet. The silk hoped for from the Huguenots had materialized to a certain extent, and better than the wine and oil they were also expected to make; the fruited mulberry sprig in a horse shoe fixed as a sort of device over the porch at Mulberry was probably something to work towards as well as a play on the name of the place, for Thomas Broughton, who built the house, was married to a daughter of old Governor Sir Nathaniel Johnson, who had named his plantation Silk Hope and fulfilled the name by producing silk upon it in commercial quantities. Indigo had been kept from popularity by the intricacies of dye making, but the war with France that made rice a drug on the Charles-Town market also cut off the English weavers from the indigo that had come to them from French Pondichery, Martinique and Monserrat, and thus gave to Carolina Low Countrymen a double incentive to turn to the cultivation of this product.

One of the most successful experimenters with indigo was a precocious girl in her teens, Eliza Lucas. Her father, the Governor of Antigua, had settled his invalid wife and their children in the healthier Low Country of Carolina, where Eliza, the eldest, had charge of their plantation. When talk of indigo began Governor Lucas sent packets of seed to his daughter and was also able to find to help her a man experienced in the tricks of making the dye, a task of great delicacy. Any fair planter with the average gang of hands could make the weed, but training and organization of master and men were extremely necessary once the mass of green leguminous stuff was cut. The quality and price of the manufactured dye varied widely and it took a split-second judgment as to just when to stop the "steeping" or the "beating" of the liquor and when to let in the lime-water that precipitated the "mud," as each step might settle the question whether you got something that remained truly little better than mud or the *fine purple*, the *fine copper*, or the most-to-be-desired *fine flora* of the trade.

Eliza Lucas, with the aid of her assistant and the coöperation of a neighbor, Andrew Deveaux, did a very great deal towards establishing the new crop. The Low Country was to be more in her debt, for she later became the mother of Thomas and Charles Cotesworth Pinckney, distinguished planter-politicians of the Revolutionary period, and of the Mrs. Horry to whom Hampton Plantation owes a graceful portico and Harrietta a very charming house.

Once indigo was established in South Carolina, the British Government, on its good old principle of Imperial Preference, put a bounty upon it that whetted the Low Country's taste for the business. Shortly, it was said, a man with any care might double his capital in five years at indigo planting. Best of all, it was an upland crop and it spread plantations into regions away from the inland swamps. It was a favorite crop of the Sea Islands and it practically settled such thriving parishes as that of St. Stephen's, whose handsome church was built by a commission made up of indigo planters, some of them among the most successful in the Low Country. It came in time too to offset the first loss of plantation regions from soil exploitation, for in the year when it was spreading new communities, such old ones as that on Goose Creek were dying, losing their people and letting their plantations start on a slow road to ruin.

Indigo prosperity, supplementing that of rice, which came back with peace, gave the Low Country its second great age of building—a time particularly of fine parish churches, but also of such eminent domestic achievements as Daniel Horry's ballroom at his "capital" mansion on Hampton Plantation and Henry Middleton's great gardens on the Ashley River. Truly it was one of the finest periods of living in a land where living had become an art, practiced on almost a European scale of culture.

Here, again, marriages give us a hint of the state and ambition of the country, for in this time two Scotch ladies, in title as well as in fact (they being the daughters of an attainted Jacobite earl), were most eagerly married up and down the Low Country, just as fast as the death of an incumbent husband gave another a chance at a titled wife. And, glory upon glory, shortly before the Revolution an Izard from Goose Creek married a daughter to a younger son of a Duke of Argyll!

But symptoms of change were already to be seen even in the architecture of the time, for however fine the work on the plantation houses, they were being quite eclipsed by contemporary Charles-Town mansions. The orientation of Low Country life was shifting subtly towards the town and towards the theories of democracy on account of which the heirs of some of the greatest Low Country estates would shortly be leading South Carolina into the Revolution.

After 1730 South Carolina's links with England had been variously strengthened. First, Englishmen like John Fenwick, enriched by a sojourn in the Low Country, and afterwards true Low Countrymen like William Middleton of Crowfield, began to go "home" (as both sorts called England) to set up there as minor nabobs. Other men, like Chief Justice Charles Pinckney, took their young children "home" to give them a completely English education. Others yet, like Gabriel Manigault, sent a son to London to eat the proper number of dinners and read the law requisite to become a barrister and so take position at the head of the Charles-Town Bar. So popular was this foundation for a Low Country career that South Carolinians for a time outnumbered all the other provincial Americans studying at the Law Courts. Some Low Countrymen also mixed their sons' education, for Henry Laurens sent his son John to study in Switzerland as well as in England and so gave him the qualifications to make his brilliant diplomatic *coup* at the Court of Versailles, in the Revolution.

The windy Whig liberalism then so current at Westminster seems to have been the greater part of the *extra curricular* study of these young South Carolinians while in London, and it sent them home primed for mischief. They found there one ready excuse, for many of the most important provincial offices were filled by placemen come to America to make their fortunes by fees and fines or else maladministering by deputy while they stayed snug in England. What added to the abuse was the feeling of trained young men that such offices should naturally have been theirs. But as most of them came of wealthy or well-to-do families it was more enthusiasm than outrage that led them, in the wake of Virginia, into open rebellion. The planter class of the Low Country were far from being happy or undivided in their allegiance to such leaders, but the compact, instructed and able pressure group the young men formed, aided by men with real grievances and egged on by a small mob of Charles-Town demagogue-mechanics, like a team of run-away colts, dragged their elders into the war by the onrush of their excitement.

Charles-Town, after a fine frenzy of mob violence, had the great misfortune to see one of the first decisive American victories won in her harbor. In the June of

1776 a British squadron, which should have sailed into the harbor and taken the town, stopped on their way to pound to pieces a half-finished fort on Sullivan's Island and was itself repulsed with heavy losses.   The fight gave South Carolina her device of a palmetto, from the logs the fort was made of.   If served to give the United States its Declaration of Independence, which the Convention in Philadelphia showed a marked disinclination to sign until cheered on to the act by news of this victory. But worst of all for the Low Country, it gave the Revolutionists an idea that they could lick something more than their weight in British Grenadiers.

The first distinct reversal of this opinion came to the Low Country in the late spring of 1779, when a British force under Prevost raided up from east Florida, spread a band of destruction through the wealthy southern parishes and came within an ace of taking Charles-Town.   Though the town was saved, the enemy literally at its gates were able to take their time in retreating across the Sea Islands, devastating as they went.   Three thousand Negroes sold into the West Indies and a thousand more lost on the way were only a part of the first installment then paid by the Low Country for its young men's ideals; thoroughbred horses from plantation studs, plate from planters' sideboards, made also fairly considerable items of loss; and on top of these was added the wanton destruction of churches burned like Sheldon and a string of houses destroyed like that of John Gibbes at the Grove on Charles-Town Neck.

South Carolina began to pay a second installment of destruction in 1780.   In the spring a large British force was landed on John's Island, whence it took the Neck. A fleet was run in past the fort on Sullivan's Island, and Charles-Town, with most of the military forces of the state in its defences, was ignominiously taken after a short sharp siege.   In the two years that followed, the state in general, the Low Country in particular, suffered from the systematic plunderings of the British, from the bitternesses and horrors of a civil war, conducted largely by partisans, full of reprisals and revenges.

When there was again peace it was estimated that at least 25,000 Negroes had been lost by the Low Country.   Great areas of land were so fought over that not even wild animals survived in them; the Middle Beat of St. John's Parish had been a great country for cattle and horses, but Moultrie riding back to his North Hampton Plantation near Pinopolis found nothing alive in it but buzzards, until in his own yard he came on some of his Negroes who had managed to escape British raiders.

The Low Country paid for the war in living men as well as dead.   There were few families of any consequence that were not divided, and a considerable body of Loyalists, many of them people of ability and substance, left the state at the end of the war forever.

Its architecture suffered.   Goose Creek Church, because the arms of England had been left above the chancel, was spared indignity, but every other parish church was profaned in one way or another by the invaders and the meeting houses of the Dissenters were treated even worse. In the rough and tumble of partisan warfare houses were made to pay for their masters' behavior or opinions and were burned as examples or in vengeance. Many were hurt or destroyed in purely military operations, as a brick house was the favorite center for a defensive action. One formed the rallying point of the British line at Eutaw Springs. Biggin Church, on its convenient hill, seems to have been frequently used as a depot for stores or as a barrack. Fine houses such as that of the Colletons at Fairlawn Barony were burned in the fighting; others, like that of another branch of the family at Wadboo Barony, were allowed after the war to tumble down, when the property that had supported them had been sequestered and sold off in small tracts.

On top of all the other losses was that of the British market and bounty for indigo, for the dye-stuff was now no more popular in England than that of the French and the bounty that had made it almost unfailingly profitable was gone for good. Plantation communities like the one that had built St. Stephen's Church were abandoned. Land in them was often left to go back to the state or to be taken by squatters. "Capital" or "commodious" or merely "convenient" plantation houses (a great many of them of brick), sometimes even after persistent advertisement of sale in the Charles-Town papers, were allowed simply to fall to pieces. To look over the offers of sales of houses in the files of the *Gazette* for the last decade of the eighteenth century is somewhat of a revelation, if you know at all the swamps and wildernesses where they once stood and where it would now seem not even a Red Indian had ever had a cabin of bark.

In those days, except on certain favored rivers, the plantation system became so generally unprofitable in the Low Country that men were able to see it with some perspective and discuss for a brief while, frankly, its manifest disadvantages. In Charles-Town the abolition of slavery was openly advocated, not for what it did to the Negro but for what it did through him to the land and to the people who owned it.

Last, but by no means least, the Low Country found that it was no longer South Carolina and that South Carolina was no longer a money-making province of a great commercial empire, but one of a confederation of states whose growing democracy, having the power to tax, had also the power to destroy. Charles-Town soon after the Revolution through a new spelling of its name became Charleston. The seat of South Carolina government was transferred to the artificially created Columbia and for the next eighty-odd years Charleston had to content itself with being only the *de facto* capital of the state.

The loss of the seat of government was but one of the ways whereby the Low Country was to propitiate a semi-foreign power at its very gates. The Up Country, the hill region of the state, had been settled in part by colonies or trickles of people working into it from Charles-Town, but the largest and most dominant part of its population were contingents of Scotch-Irish Calvinists who during the middle years of the eighteenth century had made their way down through the piedmonts of Pennsylvania, Virginia and North Carolina. Up to the time of the Revolution they had been comfortably neglected by the people of the coast, but when fighting began they had to be reckoned with as both soldiers and voters. To gain their support the Low Country Revolutionists had early given up both Church Establishment and the rights of primogeniture, and the creation of a capital in the middle of the state was a further concession to a power that for the future had to be guarded against. This new régime, wherewith the young gentlemen who had studied in England would have insured the Low Country against government from London, depended on the ballot, and the ballot could now be seen as an easy way for the Up Country or the North to usurp the control the English had lost. It was, too, a sorry weapon for a region in which three men out of four were Negroes and the slave population had always outgrown the free.

The Low Country and other slave regions guarded themselves against the danger by writing into the Constitution a proviso that in counting for representation and taxation five Negro slaves would stand for three free people. The Low Country went even further, by setting up each of its parishes as a sort of planters' pocketborough, so that in the selection of a state Senate, before 1860, a Low Countryman's vote counted more maybe than those of five up-state farmers. There was besides in the Low Country the strength of communities where men had tradition behind them, education to aid them and leisure to give themselves freely to public life. Charleston, too, holding the money of the state and its business, was constantly enlisting new strength for its region by attracting ambitious and able people from abroad and from other parts of the state, and soon cotton was to give the Low Country new and unexpected aid.

Before cotton broke into the Low Country, however, rice had begun to make a new life there. Its tidal culture was apparently developed before 1783 by Gideon Dupont, of St. James', Goose Creek. This brilliant method set water to work cultivating rice on the richest procurable soil. Once proved practicable, the new method spread rapidly. The scheme depended on a habit the Low Country rivers have of cutting beds far too wide for themselves and then filling up the consequent meanders with a mixture of silt and peat; this deposit is called pluff mud, because of the blue-grey puffs, or pluffs, it sends boiling smokily up into the water when disturbed. Tides run in all Low Country rivers far higher than the "salt-points" where they cease to be brackish, and at flood tides the river waters cover the mud flats they have made. Johnstone watching these phenomena contrived a system of banks, ditches and flood gates, to make rice fields that could be kept as dry or as wet as the crop required without depending on chancy reserve waters, and which by flooding at the proper times could be freed of weeds by the simple process of drowning them and thus save a good deal of hoeing.

The method was expensive. It took a large force of hands, carefully trained, disciplined and supervised, to make it work. The clearing of the swamps and marshes was heavy labor; the building and maintenance of banks on mud that sucks down a big pine piling ten or twelve feet before the hammer touches it and that will dump a hundred-year-old bank into the river, if the current flurries the wrong way for a few hours, was a constant care and expense. However, the rewards also were somewhat superlative, for pluff-mud fields without any manuring could, and sometimes did, go on producing bumper crops for more than a century. There is a story told which seems to be as apocryphally false as to fact as it is allegorically true as to sense; according to it, a planter on the Santee Delta, where the mud is stained sanguine by red Up-Country clay, one day received a letter from an Edinburgh Writer-to-the-Signet informing him that if he would return to his ancestral Scotland and fulfill certain requirements he might become the Earl of Marchmont. The planter considered his fields from his window and wrote back that he thought it far more advantageous to himself and his heirs that he remain, as he was, a lord of marsh-mud.

Rice had won a market free from British trade restrictions by the Revolution and was soon being sent all over northern Europe. For a while it seemed to be a bonanza crop, and all that a planter needed to establish his fortune and that of his family after him was enough mud to plant it on and enough Negroes to tend the crop and keep up the banks. Where there was marsh, rice tried to go; wherever fresh water could be got to it, rice went. Marshes along reaches of river that were always deadly salt were banked in and the fields made from them were watered by elaborated systems of reserves and canals. At last planters, with the aid of a Dutch engineer, even stole fields from the back of barrier reefs, within sight and hearing of the sea itself.

The prosperity that came with these new fields was already flooding the Low Country when the one obstacle that might still have hampered the spread of the rice industry was removed. The most onerous part of making a rice crop had always been the difficult and tiresome job of husking the grain before it could be packed in tierces for the market. Much ingenuity had been spent on mechanizing the process but until 1790 no device had gotten very far from the primitive methods you may still see the Negroes using today to clean their little crops. Their machinery is a mortar burned and dug out of the end of a drum of pine log and a pestle whittled from a stick of heart pine; the power is supplied by a pair of human arms, applied with sweat and "elbow grease." Beating the tough, close-fitting chaff loose from the grain in this fashion was a heavy task that slowed down the crop's travel to market and with its monotonous drudgery took the heart out of the plantation hands. A few years after the Revolution a well-educated English millwright, Jonathan Lucas, was literally cast up into the rice-country by the sea to solve the problem, for when he was shipwrecked near the mouth of the Santee he practically found the job at his feet and there on a rice plantation he shortly perfected and set up the first successful rice-pounding mill in the Low Country.

At first Lucas' mills were worked by water and spotted about in the plantation country. Later these were supplemented by bigger mills in town. Lucas also carried his invention abroad, built mills in the Hansa towns and in England, made a fortune and founded a family whose houses and whose name are still prominent on the Santee and in Charleston.

With such an opening before them as rice gave, the great men of the new régime—the pseudo-Roman patricians of this new republic on the classic order—who deserved consular rank from their work in the Revolution and were politic enough to get it, began to build accordingly. Noble porticoes were put on the fronts of old houses, fine wings were added to the fine old work of others. New and delightful plantation houses were built with money from the rice-field mud of many rivers.

Only too soon was a fly found in this pleasant ointment—or rather a mosquito—to poison its sweetness. On the Low Country coast there had always been malaria, as there was everywhere along the Atlantic to the south of New England before the swamps were drained and the woods opened up, but in the colonial days and those of the Province the strains of germs may have been less virulent; for until the time of the Revolution, instead of shunning the country in summer, town people actually went into the swamps for campings and maroonings, to hunt deer and to fish. Perhaps the germs, like rice, in the new and favorable environments flourished more and took on greater strength. Certainly the rise of the tidal sort of rice culture seems to have definitely added to the amount, if not the actual virulence, of Low Country malaria. The change apparently came just at the time of the war, and one of the privations to which the plantation people were subjected during the British occupation was their inability to get into Charles-Town and away from the country and its fevers of the summer months. True, the town was sometimes visited by yellow fever, but because of its salt rivers and the sweep of constant breezes the slow-flying malaria-carrying mosquito never throve there.

Luckily, a few hundred millenia of life in African jungles had given the Negroes an immunity to the fever. They throve where their masters perished and they lived comfortably enough on the plantations while white men dared not be caught there within an hour of night-fall, for as long as it was broad day you were safe anywhere from the terror that flew only by night.

It was found also that the horrible miasma, as curious in its habits as a Chinese devil, did not touch you if you spent all the hours of darkness at the sea-beaches or in the pine lands away from the river swamps. Now we know that the steady landward breezes from the ocean kept the beaches clear of the carrier mosquito and that the sandy pine lands were naturally free of infection because their soil was too barren for undergrowth and too porous to hold a puddle of water long enough for a mosquito to hatch, but it was without any knowledge of the true causes of malaria that the planter people had, by the last decade of the eighteenth century, worked out through trial and error a satisfactory way of avoiding the disease.

In that ten years a number of little villages sprang up all over the plantation country. Sea-Island people chose the beaches for themselves, inlanders the pine lands, and lightly built, airy little houses with many piazzas were spotted along the sand-dunes or scattered among the pines, where the breezes of the ocean or the terebinthine odors of the pines would protect the plantation people from the night miasmas. The pines were given such credit for their control of the infection that they were treated with almost superstitious honor. In Summerville, which confesses its origin by its name, it is still unlawful for any one except the village authorities to remove a pine tree, dead or alive, and the motto of the town bids it "Keep the Pine Sacred." In Pineville the Board of Trustees of the Academy fined you for destroying a pine in any way, and even bought up farms that were considered to have brought open ground too close to the village, to let them grow up in pines again. Doubtless the records of Plantersville, Pinopolis and Summerton would show a similar regard for the trees in those topically named communities.

The summer village as it reoriented the life of the plantation people had its due effect on plantation architecture. The fever season began in May. In most of St. John's, Berkeley, the tenth of the month had a malignant significance; at any rate, before the full power of the summer sun came down on the swamps and the rice-fields the planters and their families got themselves away from the plantation houses and did not return to sleep in them until after the first killing frost of autumn blackened the sweet-potato vines. In the four or five month interval of absence the planter visited his plantation and rode his crops with more or less regularity. A properly diligent man went every working day, but it was easier and pleasanter to hire an overseer who could be paid to have the fever, live on "bark" and keep the Negroes and the crops in order, in between his chills.

This necessary removal was in itself a temptation towards more extensive absenteeism. Charleston and the charm of its life drew the plantation people constantly. A town house was the desideratum of every Low Country family that approached wealth. Once achieved, there was always increasing excuse for using the house; in the summer it gave the company of the town, as well as freedom from malaria, and in the winter of course it could be used in the social season. A man who built in town and also on his plantation would naturally set out the best where it would be most seen.

Once people were dislodged from their plantations during the summer the distance they might go was dependent only on their wealth and the ease of travel. Of course the restless rich, the natural builders of good houses and the proper prey of architects, went farthest afield. Low Countrymen discovered the Up Country physically as well as politically during the Revolution, learned the charms of the high hills with their views of the Blue Ridge Mountains, realized the pleasure of sleeping under a blanket on August nights. After the war they found their way back to summer in the Piedmont. Pleasant villages like old Pendleton became the center of Low Country summer settlements, made up of self-supporting farms where provisions were made for the summer sojourners and where gentlemen might even have orchards sufficient in extent to keep them in peach brandy the year around. The next generation, with improved methods of travel and provisioning, dared to go into the mountains they as children had viewed from the hills, and make of such places as Flat Rock sorts of summer Charlestons, strung out over agreeable mountain country.

They even traveled farther afield. With good roads family carriages accompanied by the master's gig and the sons on horseback could make their way to the Virginia Springs, and so give North Carolina a new definition as "the place you went through to get to Virginia." Some people took boat for New York and traveled up the Hudson to Balston Spa, to drink the waters, enjoy the diversions and sometimes involve themselves in flirtations that even now reëcho in the ancient *on dit* of the plantation country. Parties went farther by water, for plantation people from the Low Country were among the first to "discover" on the New England coast, which was so agreeably different from their own, two of its most famous resorts. Newport was made fashionable largely by South Carolinians who summered in the neighborhood, and sent their boys to school in the town or their consumptives to die there and to be buried in its Episcopal graveyard; and the delights of Mt. Desert were early tasted and recommended by Low Country planters.

With these extended summer holidays and the season in Charleston to take a part out of the winter, absenteeism might become so complete that a plantation house was nothing much more than a place where you spent a month at Christmas and used to go to during Lent, when dancing had ended in town and the country was lovely with spring.

The Revolution had made its differences to the planters both rich and well-to-do. Before the war, even if the law of primogeniture had never been strictly observed, it was a part of the English tradition of land-owning that had a definite appeal to Low Countrymen. As often as not, particularly in the early days, the home place went to the youngest son, the last one to be provided for; but when some magnificence had been achieved in a house or a garden, the eldest son had it set apart for him and the law of primogeniture might be invoked, if necessary, to give him the means to remain the head of the family and to keep the plantation its country seat. After the Revolution, and the loss of the law, very few men tried to peg down their posterity to any plantation, even by building a fine house on it. The land had not proved the permanent thing it had seemed at home in England. Under a republic you were not supposed to play favorites among your children. The idea of an aristocracy, too, was talked down, however much it was played up. Men built in the country for their comfort, using wood rather than brick, and the notion of a plantation as a country seat was gradually lost with the law designed to give continuity to land and blood.

Sometimes in the new days there was also a genuine feeling of republican simplicity in building. Thus Peter Gaillard, in planning a new house at the Rocks in 1804, though he was a well-to-do man at the time and on his way to be considered rich, could be careful to specify in matter of decoration that "two of the chimney pieces . . . be done in a genteel but plain style, [and the] . . . others . . . to be very plain."

The loss of Church Establishment was also hard on plantation architecture. Many of the clergy of the Low Country were Loyalists who left their parishes with the British forces. The end of official prestige took away from the importance of the churches, and their influence was lessened by the disorganization of the war and the free-thinking and deistic or agnostic morality that came in the era of the French Revolution. The disruption of plantation life by malaria moved men away from their churches in the summer, and the breaking down of communities, as at Goose Creek and St. Stephen's, left not enough people to support a church. The old buildings fell into such bad order as to be despaired of. Children grew up hardly having seen a clergyman. The idea of a church structure as an expression of community pride, and with it something of the art of building, was lost.

Later, when an evangelical movement swept the plantation people back to religion, they were only too easily content to build chapels that were as simple and utilitarian as their summer cottages. There is hardly a church built by the Episcopalians in the Low Country after the Revolution, and now extant, that is worth any particular architectural notice. The almost inclusive sect repaired burned buildings like Sheldon, but they saved notions of dignity in a new church for those in town. There St. Paul's, known as the Planters' Church from the number of them in its congregation, shows their sense of dignity and comfort in its ample proportions and their appreciation of good architecture in its handsome designing and decoration. Partly this was the question of emulation; the Presbyterian Church on Edisto, the only post-Revolutionary church illustrated in this book, would go to prove the rule, for Edisto was then not only a very wealthy community but was self-centered almost to the point of a civic consciousness, and also split between the Presbyterians and Episcopalians in just the proportions to promote rivalry in such matters as church building.

The "black seed" cotton that made the plantations whose owners built this last-mentioned church was, by that time, such a specialty of Edisto and the coastwise archipelago to the south of it as to begin to deserve their name and be called Sea-Island cotton. It is just possible that this kind of cotton was grown in the Low

Country before the Revolution, for it is known that Henry Laurens, the celebrated merchant-planter, and always an experimenter with commercial plants, in 1768 sent to the West Indies for cotton seed, where it had always been commonly grown. After the Revolution, however, just as indigo had been brought in to bolster rice in the 1740's, cotton was called in to substitute for indigo.

Green-seed cotton, a commonplace crop in the Low Country, still gave its planters the trouble of clearing it from its seed. Various attempts had been made to perfect gins that would do this work, yet until the very end of the eighteenth century the task of tearing the fiber from its closely attached seed was still hand work that occupied everybody on the plantation, from the planter's family down, white or black, young or old. The black-seed sort was less hard to clean, for its longer, silkier fiber is attached only to the end of the brown seed. It had not been used as a field crop in the Low Country until it came in from Georgia where, according to the best accounts, it had been introduced from the Bahamas about 1786 by an exiled Loyalist still patriotic enough to send its seed back to his ex-neighbors, ruined indigo planters, in the hope that it might help them to a new crop.

Until 1793 cotton of either sort seems to have done little more than put new heart into the desolated indigo country. In that year, the same in which the French rid themselves of a king, the South took one. For Whitney's gin—like black-seed cotton a product of a Georgia plantation—then began King Cotton's epic reign over the South, its delivery to a serfdom of exploitation in the rising machine age.

Everything about the act and the time was fatal. Had not some such crop come into South Carolina and Georgia just then it is possible that the plantation system, lacking an astonishingly favorable vehicle, might not have spread as it did. Instead, it might have been confined to such favorable localities as Low Country and Georgia rice-rivers or the sugar lands of Louisiana and might have kept slavery to them. Slavery as a problem of limited sections could then have met its doom quietly, perhaps at the time the British abolished it in the West Indies, or possibly it would later have died of its own toxins. But cotton fitted the requirements of the plantation system as a hand does its glove, and the gin made it in truth something more than any human tyrant could have been to the South.

Cotton's effect on the Low Country was almost immediate. Everyone not already happily attached to a rice plantation turned to it. Shortly it spilled plantations over the parish lines into what had been known as the Middle Country, making it virtually a part of the Low Country and enlarging the old city-state to something like twice its pre-Revolutionary area. This Middle land proved to be one of the best regions for cotton in the South. It had been settled partly by colonies that had arrived by way of Charleston and partly by penetrations of Low Countrymen, but most of its people had come down into it from Virginia in the middle years of the eighteenth century. Even before the Revolution the more prominent of the Middle

Country tribes had begun to make alliances with the Low Country people, and now with the growth of their plantations ties of all sorts were made between the coast and its new acquisition, giving to the planters of the second generation in what had been the Middle Country the imprint of Tide Water people.

To a certain extent cotton and the plantation system carried, wherever they spread, something of Low Country culture and blood and influence, so that long before 1860 Charleston had achieved an amazing amount of power over an astonishing part of the great territory its namesake King so long before had granted to its lordly establishers.

In the Low Country itself cotton built new regions of plantations and made over old ones left derelict by indigo, doing for sections like Upper St. John's, Berkeley, and the Sea Islands what rice had done for the Santee and the Combahee. What the crop could accomplish on an inland plantation is plainly shown by the career of Peter Gaillard, the builder of The Rocks. At the beginning of the Revolution he had come into a good indigo plantation in St. Stephen's; within ten years after the peace such places were not even making rations for their people, for in addition to the loss of indigo, the annual floodings of the Santee swamp lands where Gaillard and his neighbors had made their provision crops had robbed these planters almost of the bare necessities of living. Milford Plantation, in that neighborhood, for which Samuel Cordes had paid six thousand guineas sterling not long before the Revolution, was abandoned as simply worthless about 1790. In desperation, Gaillard in 1794 bought a tract in Upper St. John's, in the neighborhood of Eutaw Springs, solely to make food for his family and his Negroes. With Huguenot shrewdness he chose land enriched with outcroppings of soft marl (because of which he named his place The Rocks). But he was so hard-pressed by debt that had he not won a prize in the East Bay lottery in the nick of time to make a second payment on the place he must have lost it. Cotton had already been tried in the neighborhood by General William Moultrie at North Hampton Plantation, but without much success. Gaillard, however, put in a crop in 1796. By 1800 he was out of debt. By 1803 he was building the big substantial house at The Rocks, getting it finished in time for the first marriage of one of his children. By 1828, when he gave up his "planting operations and continued to live in Charleston" in a house on upper East Bay, he had paid $118,000 for real property, reared over four hundred Negroes, settled a plantation on each of his five sons and town houses on each of his three daughters and kept besides a tidy little fortune to see him through his old age.

But cotton peculiarly blessed the Sea Islands. The black-seed kind, of tropic origin, never lost some of its tropic delicacy; it had a taste for insularity and relished the neighborhood of the salt streams. These protected it from cold at the beginning of spring, and gave it leisure to develop its great growth of "weed" (tall sometimes as a man on horse-back) and the silken luxury of its fiber. Sea-Island planters became expert at the art of indulging it, breeding their strains of its seed as suited their tastes, rearing plants as specialized as thoroughbred horses. Islands, families or plantations became famous for the peculiar virtues of their cotton and the peculiar values they got for it. And all this happened within two generations of the time that men had seen nearly the complete ruin of these islands with the passage of indigo.

The house William Seabrook built on Edisto at the beginning of the nineteenth century marks the arrival of Sea-Island cotton prosperity; the Presbyterian Church and the well-planned Launch house on the same island show its continuity, but even while these last were being built the centripetal drag of Charleston was making itself seen in the architecture here as everywhere else in the old Low Country.

As Seabrook's plan became a prototype for other builders we see a close resemblance between it and two of its derivatives. One of these was built by Seabrook's son at Oak Island about 1830, the other some dozen years later by I. Jenkins Mikell at Peter's Point. In each there seems to be a progressive regard for solid comfort at the expense of design. The point is clearly illustrated in the matter of piazzas: Seabrook's double-tiered portico, direct in its apostolic succession through Drayton Hall from Scamozzi and Palladio, is a handsome, decorous equivalent to them; but at his son's place, though much attention was given to an extensively elaborate garden, the house is hedged half about with a piazza of a usual and cumbersome Charleston type. And Mikell at Peter's Point, though he placed his house to overlook St. Helena's Sound, one of the noblest seascapes of the section, covered its front with a double-decker piazza that is as uncompromisingly overwhelming as any in the Low Country.

A comparison of Mikell's house with the town mansion he built a little later would seem to show that by then a plantation house had become a residence for the working part of the year, specialized for that function only in a more elaborate degree than were the camp-cottages at the beaches or in the pine lands. Mikell's town house, once occupied by the Charleston Free Library, is impressively ornate in its scale and its surroundings; its wide portico of six heroic Corinthian columns and its garden make it one of Charleston's prime examples of the classic revival of the splendid idle '50's. You can find plantation houses as grandiose as this on South Carolina plantations, but you must look for them in the Low Country's newer acquisition. There is one at Millford, near Sumter, built by John L. Manning, one of the long dynasty of Manning and Richardson governors of South Carolina; another, left in ruins by Sherman's Army, is at Millwood, the home of the second and third Wade Hampton, near Columbia, but both of these are well up in the penumbra of Charleston's influence on house builders.

Even the rice-millionaires of the coast did not deign to build notably outside of Charleston. Nathaniel Heyward, the most outstanding example of the class, who shared among his children during his life and at his death some twenty-three hundred Negroes and sixteen plantations, though he was never given to absenteeism and though his in-laws, the Manigaults, had a strong sense of architectural fitness, seems to have been content with such houses as he found on his plantations or those he built upon them in utilitarian fashion. Governor William Aiken, another great rice planter, might have had nearly a thousand Negroes on his Jehossee Island but he was satisfied with a comfortably simple house there. Both he and Heyward saved their architectural displays for the town, where Aiken's big residence still stands looking down the row of houses he is said to have built to support it, and where the remains of Heyward's house, butchered past recognition, still give a small idea of its considerable size, its interesting planning and its handsome appointments.

But however much Charleston may have taken away from the ornateness of plantation life, plantations and their owners continued to hold sway over the town, for from the plantations stemmed the real power of the Low Country. The planters dominated the politics that chose the leaders for the city-state which the parishes formed with Charleston—leaders who for good or evil held the balance of strength in the state and sent thence to Washington men who kept South Carolina in the forefront of Southern affairs. So it was that the Low Country planters largely kept the initiative in the South's long fight for self-determination, and hence it came that the issue between the agressive North and the defensive South was fairly joined by South Carolina in the nullification of a Federal tariff, in 1832, and brought at last to the opening of its fiery solution by a Secession Convention that met in Charleston and by the first guns of the Confederate War fired at Fort Sumter and over Charleston harbor.

The Low Country in the destruction of its architecture paid a full share of the cost of war during the Confederacy, as it had done in the Revolution. In part the region was in the enemy's hands from 1861, for in the autumn of that year Port Royal was carried by a Federal fleet and the nearby islands were taken and thenceforth held by them. The Sea Islands, thus made untenable, stood for a while as a sort of No-Man's-Land between the armies of the Confederacy on the mainland and the Federal flotillas that blockaded the coast and made occasional raids up its rivers. In that time such houses as William Seabrook's saw strange adventures and suffered curious dilapidations at the hands of foraging parties. Later still these houses were occupied by Federal troops as they advanced along the islands to the siege of Charleston. In the first days of 1865 Sherman, turning from the sea, marched his army through the southern end of the Low Country, making highly unprofitable architectural research in the greater part of the plantation country below the Edisto. On the night Columbia was burned Charleston was evacuated, and the forces of the Confederacy, moving towards the last battles in North Carolina, left the Low Country bare and undefended. Bodies of Federals then coming in from the coast raided through the plantation country, spotting it with ruins, turning loose in it wandering, raiding bands of demoralized freedmen, some of whom even tore down houses and carried away the material of which they had been built. Peace when it came found many a big house turned into a communal dwelling by the plantation Negroes and half wrecked in the process.

In the grim poverty and wholesale demoralization that followed the war many houses were simply abandoned, to perish by slow dilapidation or burn in forest fires. Later the Low Country began to revive. Rice again made money on the rivers and cotton on the islands, but it was noticed that without the discipline of slavery Negro labor fell off steadily in quality, and by the time those trained before the war had died or grown old, rice had become a chancy crop. Western states, too, began to grow it on lands far easier to cultivate than marsh-fields, where every storm-tide threatened breaks with which unskilled labor and impoverished planters could no longer cope. The occasional West Indian hurricanes that come upon the coast, always most unwelcome visitors, were now so many strokes of Fate; each left stretches of banks too far ruined to be recuperated. At last the planters found it easier and cheaper to keep on moving from plantation to plantation or river to river than to stay in one place and fight the hopeless battles of the broken banks. So the crop died, until at the time the first photographs for this book were taken only two or three plantations in all the Low Country were still growing rice.

Cotton fared somewhat better than rice, though it had many of the same troubles. The Sea-Island crop did moderately well for most of its planters until the coming of the boll weevil, when suddenly the always delicate, always fastidious, crop disappeared from its islands as if witched away by black magic.

For the better part of the decade that followed the World War the Low Country was a region of deserted fields growing up in forest, of ragged dying gardens and grim, cold, pathetic houses, solemnly awaiting their doom by fire or dilapidation. But with the coming of the automobile and the good roads it demanded the country was rediscovered. The wealth of post-war days set men to searching for game preserves and winter homes. The ruined rice-fields and cotton lands gave these seekers land to hunt over, the plantation houses furnished them homes already equipped with the charm of time. In a few years after this book was begun, many a house that then seemed *in extremis* was brought back to sound usefulness. Certain plantations were put to work again, and many took on new leases of life under the new dispensation.

At the beginning of the 'Forties the vast hydro-electric development started to carry off the waters of the Santee into the Cooper. The project flooded two large areas that fell within the notice of this book. The sites of six houses it illustrated were included. Of these the most were taken down, but in each instance the ornamental wood work was saved. Since then a good deal of this has been used happily by the same families for whom it was first carved and installed. Two houses we described were saved *in toto*. Mr. J. Rutledge Connor was able to carry The Rocks house to another site on his property. Hanover was rebuilt and restored, as an historic and architectural monument, near South Carolina's only School of Architecture, at Clemson College. And Woodlawn, which was too far gone for photography in 1928, was taken to Dover Plantation by Mrs. Henry Manning Sage of Albany, N. Y., and has since been rebuilt to overlook Winyah Bay.

With the second World War industry definitely moved into the South Carolina Low Country. What effects this will have upon the architecture we have described is a question to be asked of the future. While the answer is being made, it is all the more gratifying to preserve in this book a further record of a way of life as well worth remembering for the things it created as for the history it made.

ARCHITECTURAL TRENDS

I N preparing this book it was hoped that credit might be given to the architects or designers of these churches and houses; but, as you will see by reference to the particular accounts of them, when, as most rarely, any records are in existence, they are peculiarly oblivious of anything concerning the designing of the work, however careful they may be to state by whom it was carried out. It is known that competent carpenter-builders were coming into the Province from abroad in the middle part of the eighteenth century, but there is no document, so far as we have been able to determine, which connects with plantation houses any of those known to have worked in Charleston.

Even in the questions of the owners who put up the houses and the date of their construction we have frequently found ourselves at a loss. Then tradition, checked however by the interior evidence of the decoration and counterchecked by such substantiating or annulling facts as could be found in muniments, public records and genealogies, has had to be relied on. In this work the South Carolina Historical and Genealogical Magazine has proved invaluable and in it especially the work of the late Judge H.A.M. Smith and its able editor, Miss Mabel L. Webber.

In general there are several seemingly notable things about the Low Country plantation houses, among them their planning. Before the Revolution, most particularly for the length of the territory we cover, and from the opening years of the eighteenth century almost to its ending, one plan was used over and over again with only a slight variation. In point of time we find it first at Mulberry, where, if you will imagine away the towers, you have the scheme that is repeated at Hanover, Brick House, Fenwick Hall, Crowfield, Limerick and Lewisfield; at Fairfield and Hampton in their first condition; and after the Revolution at Eutaw. With its unequal division of the front of a house, and the central stair hall, it is also the plan of the upper story of the Charleston Double Houses—the scheme of most of the finer houses of the 1750's and '60's now found in the city.

In a manner the plan of Medway is a forerunner of this one. Similarly, that of Exeter, with its H shape, is an amusing variation on Mulberry with its towers, and a link of a sort from Mulberry towards the expansive planning of Drayton Hall.

Middleburg, as a foreshadowing of the classic Charleston Single House, is particularly to be noticed as an historic plan.

After the Revolution we find definite temporal and local schools of planning. In the 1790's El Dorado and Harrietta, with their elaborated wings, mark attempts to give with some architectural distinction more and better spaces for windows and the cross ventilation so necessary to comfort in the Low Country. Several other houses, also in ruins, have the general scheme of El Dorado, notably one built of tabby by the Sams family on Dawtaw Island near Beaufort.

There was also quite a vogue about this same time, both in the town and on the plantations, for the polygonal rooms made popular by the designs of the brothers Adam. Interesting variations on their schemes are to be found at Fenwick Hall, Mount Hope, The Elms, The Grove and in the wings of The Wedge.

Just about 1800 two regional plans seem to have developed that continued in use to the end of the plantation era. One of these is illustrated by the plan of Springfield, which without its wings is typical of the houses of St. John's, Berkeley, more especially those of Upper St. John's. There it is found at Belvidere Plantation, The Rocks, Lawson's Pond and Walnut Grove, and in Middle St. John's at Ophir. The odd sort of paired front doors that go with this plan, with the "Lady or the Tiger" effect on any one coming into these houses for the first time, is shown very well in the photograph of Lawson's Pond; it was to avoid just such an effect that the interesting false door was sandwiched in between such a pair at Harrietta.

William Seabrook's House, as we have noted elsewhere, was in a way the prototype of the future buildings on Edisto, the type of the Low Country's other definite regional plan.

In the matter of design the Low Country seems to have followed those current in England, with a differencing caught from the West Indies. As we have commented in the description of Goose Creek Church, it might be set down in either Antigua or Barbadoes and seem not the least out of place. The use of stucco ornament seems to have been fairly popular in the Low Country in the early eighteenth century, to judge by old descriptions of the first house at The Elms, built in 1711, and by photographs of Archdale Hall on the Ashley, a small house of considerable distinction that was ruined by the earthquake of 1886. This home of the Baker family was built of brick very much in the fashion of the minor works of Wren and its interiors were decorated with royal coats of arms and other stucco work in high relief.

Direct borrowings from Charleston work are to be noted in the ceiling at St. Stephen's Church and in the chancel and pulpit at Pompion Hill, all obviously imitated from those of St. Michael's Church in the city.

It is also interesting to note the variations on the gouge work so lavishly used at Marshlands and so beautifully executed there. As the fashion for it spread inland it seems to have varied in artfulness directly with its distance from Charleston and to have arrived at a lavish degree of popularity in the neighborhood and era of Springfield.

The idea of the piazza seems to have come from the West Indies to the Low

Country, but its evolution may be plainly seen in this book.   From the little porches at Mulberry and Brick House, it passes through the more expanded ones at Fairfield and on the garden side of Harrietta, and thence to the entrance porch on the other side of Harrietta and the portico at Lowndes' Grove, both of which are nothing but piazzas slightly disguised by pediments.   The straightforward piazza as used in Barbadoes and the Low Country may be noted on the house at Lewisfield and, later, on that at Somerset.   As well adapted to the scheme of houses, you will find them at Dean Hall and at The Launch, and at Tom Seabrook's you can see how they were only too often allowed to swarm over Low Country houses of all sorts with the exuberant inclusiveness of wild figs strangling jungle trees.

For those who care for the minutiae of evolutionary processes there should be considerable interest in the variety of the styles of the supporting posts and columns of the piazzas and porticoes on the buildings.   Leaving aside those in the classic proportions, such as the imported columns in Portland stone at Drayton Hall, those in brick at Sheldon and St. James, Santee, and those in stucco at The Elms and Chachan, we have here another succession of changing shapes.   They begin logically with the posts to the piazzas at Middleburg, which are square to the height of the porch rail and, above that, rounded and shaped crudely to the proportions of columns.   Others like this are found on early houses about Charleston and most commonly in Bridgetown, Barbadoes.   Next to them in the Low Country progression are the square wooden posts at Brick House and Mulberry, which are channeled, capped and based with a pretty careful attention to classic requirements.   There follow any number of wooden variations on those requirements in slim round posts of early piazzas, on all the little porticoes, so popular during the 1790's, and in the heroic adaptation of a stone portico into wood at Hampton.   With the coming of Adam detail, wood columns slimmer than any of these last, but square and worked to a careful entasis, begin to be used, particularly in St. John's, Berkeley, and may be seen in a robust mood on the entrance porch at Harrietta.   These are followed by polygonal columns, also given careful entasis, such as those shown in the photographs of The Grove and Somerton. And at last, on The Launch and Tom Seabrook's, you will find the stock design for piazza posts that came to the Low Country with the Greek Revival and lasted on with little variation for the rest of the plantation times.

COLONIAL AND PROVINCIAL PERIOD

MEDWAY 1686   This house on the Medway or Back River was built by Jan Van Arrsens, Seigneur de Weirnhoudt, who led a small company of Hollanders to Carolina. Shortly after his arrival he died and his widow, Sabina de Vignon, married Thomas Smith. Enriched by Van Arrsens' property Smith later became a cacique, landgrave and governor of Carolina. Through his first wife (for Sabina brought him no children) he has become one of the greatest common ancestors of the Low Country. He lies buried at Medway.

That the influence of Van Arrsens' architecture, though thoroughly encisted in additions, has kept this house looking as if it had as good right to be standing over a canal in the Low Countries of Holland as beside rice fields in the Low Country of South Carolina is a triumph of style over circumstance; for, consciously or otherwise, this Dutch builder's taste has dominated that of the succeeding owners of Medway. Whoever placed a second story on the original building obviously copied its stepped gables, and though these were thrown down in the earthquake of 1886 the late Samuel Gaillard Stoney, with the aid of old pictures, was able piously to replace them twenty years afterwards. And whoever added the low, spreading wings on the river front was sufficiently infected with the feeling of the old work to make his own seem a part of it. Even Peter Gaillard Stoney's unsymmetrical wing, built out towards the avenue in 1855, ties in with the style of Van Arrsens' building, and a very thorough recent changing of the simple interior has been effected also without any great difference to the outer look of the old house.

Medway, built only sixteen years after the founding of the colony, and now the oldest house in South Carolina of record, is in plan and situation already pretty typical of the plantation houses to be built in the Low Country during the next hundred years. The sort of Janus-like, facing-both-ways scheme entailed on a house with a river prospect and an entrance on the land side, common to the region, shows itself already here at Medway. The direct entrance into a large hall, the principal room in the house that takes a lion's share of the house front, is another characteristic that remained in vogue to the time of the Revolution.

Van Arrsen's "home-made" brick is characteristically bad. So bad that his walls were reputed to stand by the strength of the oyster shell mortar only. The stuccoing was an obvious attempt to remedy, or at least mitigate, this failing. It also is typical of early work. In the additions the brick is much improved. Back River, that flows by this plantation, was at first also called Medway. Like its English cognominant, it is banked with good clay, and lined with the remains of defunct brick-yards. These once supplied Charleston with the best grade of "Carolina Grey" brick. At Parnassus, down stream from Medway, Zachary Villepontoux made excellent brick to build St. Michael's. In the nineteenth century Medway itself enjoyed a sound economic mixture of agriculture and industry by making rice while the weather was hot and brick when it was cold. Peter Gaillard Stoney sent thousands of the latter down to the building of famous Fort Sumter.

The house has two extra-architectural claims to fame. Modified to his purpose, John Bennett made it the scene of his novel, "The Treasure of Peyre Gaillard". And here, after the second World War, was developed the celebrated "Medway Plan", for American cities to adopt French towns and help to rehabilitate them.

Medway's older plantings come from three women of the Marion-DuBose-Stoney connection that owned the place nearly a century and a quarter. Mrs. DuBose, after 1825, planted the larger oaks about the house. Her sister, Mrs. Peter Gaillard Stoney, planted the avenues in 1855. And Louisa Cheves Stoney, after 1905, restored old gardens and planted new ones, notably, the terraced lawn between the avenues with its framing of azaleas.

Sidney and Gertrude Sanford Legendre, after 1930, added very extensively to the gardens and the out buildings. He was buried here in a part of the garden of his making, near the tomb of the Landgrave and probably as close to Van Arrsen's lost grave.

Medway is the winter home of Mrs. Sidney J. Legendre.

MIDDLEBURG
1699

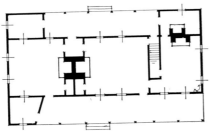

Benjamin Simons, one of several Huguenots who settled in the neighborhood of Pompion Hill, sufficiently completed the house he built there on his Middleburg Plantation to have the fifth of his fourteen children born in it during the spring of 1699. Since that time Middleburg, now become one of the oldest, if not the oldest, of the wooden houses in South Carolina, has never been out of the possession of one or another of Benjamin Simons' numerous descendants.

The northern end of the house appears to be an addition; the principal rooms downstairs were redecorated about 1800. Otherwise Middleburg is much as its builder left it and gives us an interesting combination of details European, West Indian and Carolinian. The planning of rooms, put as it were end to end so as to give them chances to catch breezes from as many directions as possible, and the use of the shading piazzas, make Middleburg the nearest approach to a prototype of the Low Country "single" house, so popular in Charleston and found nowhere else north of the Antilles. The scheme used in the older rooms of plastering the exterior walls and making the others of vertical boarding, nailed to framing with beaded edges that mortise into the floor boards, is also typical of early work in the Low Country and of old and recent work in Barbadoes. It is reminiscent of contemporary European building that the very heavy corner posts and wall beams in the framing should project into the corners of the rooms and along the top edges of their outer walls. This trick was continued in the neighborhood both at Limerick and, nearly a century later, at Hyde Park Plantation. It is exactly in keeping with the Jacobean period of this house that the bedroom fireplace should be framed with a bolection moulding, composed with pioneering ingenuity of a half-round moulding planted on a board with moulded edges. And it is typical of early Low Country work that the chimney breast above that fireplace should be finished with a panel of plastering applied directly to the brick, which eliminates a favorite place for destructive fires to start.

The outside kitchen and the offices with their cottage architecture date from the middle part of the nineteenth century.

Middleburg has a formal garden directly to the rear of the house, now full of old exotics, among them a splendid alley of very large *Camellia japonicas*.

Middleburg is now the winter residence of Edward von S. Dingle, noted painter of North American birds, whose late wife, the former Marie Guerin Ball, was a direct descendant of the Simons builders of the old house.

ST. ANDREWS' CHURCH 1706

St. Andrew's Parish, taking in a good part of the Ashley River with its early and fine plantations, was once one of the richest and most important in the Low Country. The walls of the nave of its cruciform church are now the oldest architecture of the Episcopal Establishment in South Carolina. An inscription incised in a red tile over the end of the transept that looks towards Ashley River records that the building was begun in 1706, the year the parish was established, *J. F.* (for Jonathan Fitch) and *T. R.* (for Thomas Rose) being the *Supervisors*.

In 1723 the transepts and choir were added to the original building, giving it the present shape. The church was burned to its walls in 1764, and built back into them. In 1855 the fittings and decorations, as their style testifies, were fashionably renewed.

This part of the old parish kept its name when it was made a township. Here one of the most populous of Charleston's numerous suburbs has grown up. The church became active again. In 1949 it was thoroughly rehabilitated, and in the year 1955 it resumed full parish status.

ST. JAMES' CHURCH, GOOSE CREEK
1708

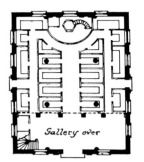

Gallery over

Goose Creek Church has several claims to Low Country fame. It is the place of worship of what was the earliest Anglican congregation in the colony outside of Charleston—the congregation of the Barbadians, the Goose Creek Men, who were the first of the Low Country's planter people, the backbone of the party that established the Church of England in the Province—and it is the best preserved, and in some ways the most interesting, of the older parish churches.

The first of many missionaries sent to South Carolina by the Society for the Propagation of the Gospel, the Rev. Samuel Thomas, served this congregation. Another, the Rev. Francis Le Jau, D.D., became first rector of the parish. The church begun under him has long since become a monument to its preservers as well as its creators. Worn lands, the Revolution and malaria combined so to deplete the congregation that since the beginning of the nineteenth century the church has been virtually dormant. Its vestries, assisted by individuals and organizations have repaired decays and such disastrous damages as were worked by the great earthquake of 1886. The walls of very soft brick continuously settled and fissured until in 1955 a substitution of massive concrete footings cured the trouble. Five years later the exterior was restored, following the earliest known picture of the building, a little water-color, sketched about 1800, by the 'prentice hand of Charles Fraser, later the celebrated miniaturist. Quiescence has in large part preserved this distinguished little building.

The decoration and fitting of the chancel are an interesting gloss on late Stuart Anglicanism. The pulpit's position is typical of the time. It is puritanical, directly before the center of the East window, emphasizing the evangelical trend and at the same time precluding an altar. And back of it the reredos, with composite pilasters, broken and curved pediment, and the arms of George I, comes about as close to Jesuit baroque as was reached in the Thirteen Colonies.

The planter aristocracy of the congregation sport their heraldry from 1719 forward. The hatchment on the front of the gallery is attributed to several of the many Ralph Izards, who once worshipped and now lie buried here. The most probable candidate died in 1743.

The little church is an awful warning to the consistent. The cornices above the outer doors depend in part for definition on the difference in their color from that of the walls. The tall wooden colonnades within the building run at both ends into windows. The floor of the gallery, first designed for parishioners unable to afford pews, later given over to colored people, had to be jerried over the front door. But with all these egregious neglects of proper designing the building's charm carries our minds and eyes past and over its failings.

When the Parish came into existence with the Church Act of 1706, measures were soon taken to replace a wooden church of sorts with something more fitting the dignity of the chief proponents of the Establishment. Materials for this church were being collected in 1707. Building was begun in 1708. But Queen Anne's War slowed the work, probably. And the Yemassee War of 1715 came into the parish and nearly made an end to it. The church was finished, at last, in 1719. According to custom, the vestry then distributed, or sold, the pews and paid the bills. And in the case of St. James', Goose Creek, they also consecrated the church building, solely to religious use, by their own resolution.

MULBERRY 1714

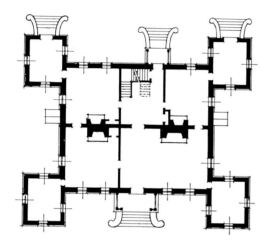

Mulberry is the only representative of a fair sized group of "mansions", built with the first crop of Low Country fortunes in the opening years of the eighteenth century. Thomas Broughton, by 1714, was a quite successful man, with a mixed career that comprised Indian trading, planting, soldiering, and office holding. He was married to the daughter of Sir Nathaniel Johnson, of Silk Hope, who had been governor both of Antigua (with the Leewards) and Carolina. Broughton was himself to be a governor here later on. This house was obviously intended as a seat, not only for its builder but for untold generations of Broughtons.

With this in their minds the romantics of the nineteenth century called the place Mulberry Castle. But though through the Yemassee War the house served as the center of a fortification mounting cannon, the little pseudo-military towers with their large windows were put there purely for ornament and ostentation, ripe bits of the ripe Jacobean baroque style in which the house was designed.

The principal rooms of the house were obviously redecorated at the end of the eighteenth century when yields from the old fields of Mulberry Swamp were being supplemented by the rice from the marsh fields along the river. But in the second story under the broad gambril roof with its jerkin-headed gables, the bedrooms have kept the doors with odd-shaped panels and heavy moulding and the chimney places framed with bolections that belong with the towers and the taste of the old house.

Mulberry was excellently restored after 1915 for the late Clarence E. Chapman by Charles Brendon, an architect from England practicing in this country. A most interesting replacement was the device of an oversized, fruited, mulberry twig, framed in a horse shoe. This piece of wood carving, found broken in the garret of the house, has been placed in the pediment of the entrance porch, where its omen for luck should do the most good.

One of the great charms of Mulberry is its situation on a high bluffed hill that gives fine views of the Western Branch of the Cooper and its rice fields. Because of a mulberry growing prominently in the Indian plantation which then crowned the hill the first Carolinians called the spot the Mulberry Tree. It was choice enough to be set aside once for a plantation for the Earl of Shaftesbury. Later it was included in the Fairlawn Barony taken up by Sir Peter Colleton, the second Baronet and Proprietor. Whether Thomas Broughton got it for his house somewhat by *force majeur* (as he once attempted to take the governorship of the Province) is now a question in archeological casuistry not to be entered into here, but it is of record that he had built upon this splendid site some time before he owned it.

This house is most definitely dated by figures cut through the iron work of the weather vanes on the four towers. It is remarkable for being one of the few buildings of brick laid up in English bond now standing in the Low Country outside of Charleston.

The grounds about the house were very handsomely landscaped for Mr. and Mrs. Chapman by Loutrel W. Briggs, of Charleston.

Mulberry is now the home of Mrs. Marion Brawley.

HANOVER 1720

Most of the Huguenots for a generation after they came to South Carolina kept somewhat on the wing, removing from neighborhood to neighborhood in bettering their lands as they bettered their conditions. Just about the time that the House of Hanover came to the throne, Paul de St. Julien, who built this house and gave his plantation its topical name, with a considerable company of his relatives and co-religionists took up grants or bought land along the rich inland swamps that drain from the Middle Beat of St. John's, Berkeley, into the Cooper. The neighborhood was so continuously predominated by their descendants thereafter that up to a few years ago two men of unmixed Huguenot blood, the last of their kind in the Low Country, still planted there. The house at Hanover represents the achievement of a people who had come from persecution, started at scratch in a new country and, in the face of prejudice, come to prosperity. St. Julien, with a truly Gallic appreciation of these facts, engraved in the stucco band at the top of one of his massive chimneys the words *PEU À PEU*, the beginning of the old French saying, *Peu à peu l'oiseau fait son nid*. The nest he built so solidly remained in his family until it was sold by Mrs. John St. Clair White nearly two hundred years later.

Hanover has a plan obviously akin to those of Medway and Mulberry. As at Middleburg, all the interior partitions of this house are made up of vertical boarding. In the principal room these are matched together with concealed jointing and then covered with applied styles and rails that cut them up into panels. In the upper story the undersides of the Dutch roof are ingeniously ceiled with planking lapped like weather-boarding, but in reverse, so that any water that penetrates to it will be run down into the eaves. The partitions in this story are rabbetted so that the alternate planks project and give a most interesting sort of corduroy look to the walls. But the chimneys are in many ways the most notable features of the house; built of large, roughly made brick in colors running from soft golden browns to quiet purples, they are of a construction downright Gothic in its functionalism. Not a brick has been wasted, from the deep basement to the flue tops, and every movement of a flue is confessed by a shoulder or an inset. Next to his motto they are the most Gallic things about Paul de St. Julien's work.

Hanover was the most interesting and valuable of a score of old houses that had to be gotten out of the way of the great Santee-Cooper Project. This is the oldest of six that we will note. Realizing that this old house was, architecturally speaking, very truly an historic monument, it was carefully taken down, and reconstructed at Clemson College where South Carolina's only School of Architecture is located. The work was done by the college's own force of builders, most ably directed by its Superintendent of Buildings and Grounds, Mr. David J. Watson.

When this work was done, it was discovered that from framing, to flooring, to shingles all the wood work of Hanover was cypress.

CHRIST CHURCH
1724

Christ Church Parish has suffered always in its churches. The first, built in 1707 shortly after the Establishment, was burned in 1724. The next, made of brick, was sufficiently complete in 1727 to be dedicated to worship, though after the leisurely fashion of the period it does not seem to have gotten its finishing touches for some time, as there is a record that in the May of 1729 "At a Vestry was ordered drawn on all yt Subscribed to ye rufcasting of ye Church."

The British burned out this building in 1782 but the walls would appear to have been rebuilt upon. In 1865 Negro Federal troops so wrecked the interior of the church that again it had practically to be rebuilt. The wooden spire, rising from the center of the church, was erected in 1835 and heightened in 1838.

In the church yard of Christ Church may be seen a Vestry, or coachman's house, used for meetings of the officers of the congregation and as a refuge on inclement

Sundays for servants who had to keep an eye upon their horses. This interesting little building was repaired lately, after having been a ruin for a great many years. It is now used as a Sunday school.

STRAWBERRY CHAPEL 1725

About five miles down the Cooper from the Mulberry, on the opposite shore, was a bluff-land called the Strawberry. This furnished the northward landing for the only practicable ferry site on this branch of the river. James Child was granted the Strawberry in 1698, started or encouraged a ferry, and in 1707 laid out a town there called Childsbury. In its plan he provided a square for a College or University, a lot for a Free School and house for the Minister and an acre and a half of land for a Church or Chapel. Of these institutions and projects the school existed for some time, but this Parochial Chapel of Ease, begun in 1725, to serve the people of the Lower Beat of the very large parish, is all that now remains of the little still-born town which soon lost even its name and left its chapel to take that of the adjacent ferry. Such chapels were of frequent occurrence in the Low Country, where the older parishes were laid out so lavishly that regular attendance at the parish church was a hardship to many. Such a fate as Childsbury's was also typical of a number of municipal projects for the Low Country, most of which never got off the parchment on which they had been planned.

Strawberry Chapel now has periodic services. Lately it repossessed the ancient Church silver of St. John's, Berkeley. In 1865 Keating Simons Ball buried it under a barn at Comingtee, to save it from the invading Federals. In some fashion the spot was never found until a mine detector was employed. Then it was brought to light again after eighty-two years of burial.

BRICK HOUSE, EDISTO 1725

Paul Hamilton, a man of great ability and circumspection, who was in turn Comptroller and Governor of South Carolina, and Secretary of the United States Navy, left a short memoir. In it, to illustrate the character of his grandfather whose name and nature he, himself, had inherited, the governor gives a short account of the building of this house. The brick was imported from Boston, where a harder and denser sort was got than any obtainable locally. Sand and gravel, free from salt, were fetched from the freshes of the Pon Pon. Lumber was cut on Hamilton's own plantations, and he suffered no wood to be used in this house that had not been housed and seasoned seven years. Since the house burned it has been found also that all his floor joists were made of oak. A very exceptional performance in a country where yellow pine was so profuse and so excellent.

The builder of Brick House was the son, and grandson, of two able and prominent colonists, John Hamilton and Paul Grimball. In the happy beginnings of the Royal Government, he prospered with a large number of other South Carolinians. There seems no way to find exactly when this house was erected, but 1725 gives a fair approximation. Hamilton died, a little beyond middle age, in 1738.

The many stucco enrichments and the high-pitched roof of Brick House gave it curiously the air of French work of the time of Henri IV or Louis XIII, a look of being distinctly related to the Place des Vosges. This quality was probably heightened by two small flankers, or pavilions, long since lost, that stood on either side of the front. And even the deep bell casting with which the roof comes down to the cornice (a trick much used in both South Carolina and the West Indies) adds to this Gallic resemblance.

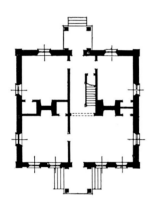

Since 1798 Brick House has been the property of the Jenkins family. Most unhappily it was gutted by fire shortly after these photographs were taken, but its owners have seen to the preservation of the stout brick walls and hope to rebuild within them.

In the hall, or principal room the woodwork was much enriched with paintings. In spite of the age and varnish that kept it from showing in the photograph, a landscape with figures could be made out in the square panel over the fireplace. The long flanking panels had pictures of fruit, including a pair of colossal bunches of grapes, like those the Israelitish spies on old tapestries bring back from the land of Canaan. The horizontal panel just above the bolection mould contained a design of rinceaux with masks, and in the square metopes of the Doric cornice that crossed what was once a framed opening to the stairway were alternately pictured, in heraldic fashion, stags' masks and roses.

E XETER 1726

Hugh Butler, husband to Anne Colleton, leased a southern part of the Fairlawn Barony of the Colletons in 1726, called it Exeter, and built upon it. This was the most probable origin of the dwelling house on this plantation, though the date of its building is subject to much local dispute, even being claimed by one owner to be as early as 1700, as is shown by the figures later cut in the chimney-cap.

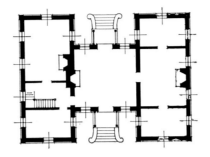

The original H-shaped plan of the house, somewhat like that of Tuckahoe in Virginia, was very much altered some time in the middle of the nineteenth century when the two wings towards the front were removed to make way for a long piazza and a stairhall was filled in between those at the rear. This has not been able to detract from the quaintly pleasing quality of the house, but its symmetry is marred and the light of its central hall is lost. Paint on the outer walls has also dimmed handsome brickwork laid in Flemish bonding with glazed headers and killed the effect of the white stucco around the bases of the walls and over their corner pilasters.

This house was long the home of the Motte family and filled with Motte, Broughton and Johnson heirlooms. It is now the home of the Berkeley Country Club.

CROWFIELD 1730

Edward Middleton and his brother Arthur came from Barbadoes to Carolina and settled on Goose Creek in the seventeenth century. There the family so flourished that in 1729 Arthur Middleton of the Oaks, son to Edward, as President of the Council was acting Governor of the Province and well able to give his son William a fair-sized plantation near his own, with ample means to improve it. This place was then named Crowfield, after an English property of their family's.

William Middleton, who married after he received Crowfield, probably proceeded at once to the building of the "Capital mansion . . . with twelve good rooms with fire places in each besides four in the basement with fireplaces," the flankers and outbuildings and the "elegant garden . . . extensively laid out in good taste with Fish Ponds and Canals superior to anything of the kind" in the Low Country.

There is a somewhat ecstatic picture given of Crowfield about 1743 by Eliza Lucas, who made a visit at the house. Writing to another young lady, she describes the mile-long avenue, the spacious basin and green before the house, the house and the gardens. She identifies for us the bowling green and the site of a thicket or bosquet of young live oaks, speaks of the double rows of large flowering "laurel" (now grown into giant and decaying magnolias) and those of catalpas, whose descendants have broken loose throughout the ruined garden. She lumps references to the mount, the wilderness and lesser garden contrivances, most of them now lost under ploughing and pine-scrub, and she grows enthusiastic upon the fine prospect from the house over the water of the large fish ponds, of smiling fields dressed in vivid green, where is now nothing but a tangle of forest.

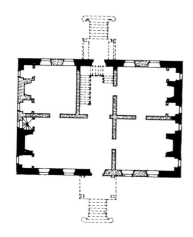

Enough of the "capital mansion" remains to show that its front and rear walls were laid up in Flemish bonding with light red stretchers and glazed headers of a purple blue (the other walls being of English bond with unglazed headers) and the house further enriched with quoinings, belt courses and voussiors in a soft yellow stucco. Within the house the plan can still be discerned and the parlor chimney still shows the scars of its tile lining, all now plucked off and carried away.

Crowfield is now the most haunting spot in the Low Country, and one of the most vivid illustrations of the changes that came over the Low Country in its first century of life, for hardly was it finished than it began to decline. In 1753 William Middleton sold it and removed to its namesake in Suffolk, which he had inherited and where his eldest son remained to become an M.P. and a baronet. Two of his sons came back to live at Crowfield on Goose Creek, one as a tenant and the other, the youngest, to buy it back into the family in 1783. By then, however, its 1800 acres, once advertised as so good for "either rice, corn, or indigo," were nearly exhausted. Thomas Middleton, John's cousin, was soon after selling the old home at the Oaks and wisely seeking new lands, and though the Middletons kept Crowfield for more than a century thereafter, the expensive house and expansive garden were allowed to go gradually to ruin along with the unprofitable fields that surrounded them.

The restoration here of the garden, although accurate as to the still discernible earthworks and buildings, is of necessity somewhat free in detail. The fish ponds, which seem also to have furnished water for the rice fields below them, have long since been drained for the sake of their fish. Adventurers have dug down through the mount in the garden hunting treasure. What remains of the avenue still contains some of the finest live oaks for shape in the Low Country, but they are badly overgrown with holly and dogwood. And even if in the mind's eye it still contrasts well with the preserved splendors of Middleton Place, made by William's brother Henry on the Ashley, Crowfield is lost in a lost country. It is the property now of the West Virginia Pulp and Paper Company.

FENWICK HALL 1730   Fenwick Hall marks the cresting of a wave of prosperity that came over the Low Country in the decade after the end of the Proprietorial Government with its last complications of Indian wars and piratical incursions in the Low Country proper. The house also signifies the arrival at considerable wealth of an interesting family. Robert Fenwick, one of the "Red Sea Men" who upon their arrival in Carolina on the priva-

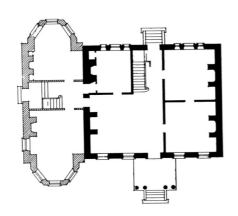

teer *Loyal Jamaica* were bonded to behave themselves during their sojourn, came of a good, sometimes prominent, county family in England. John Fenwick followed his elder brother to the Province, where he shortly prospered exceedingly in business, in politics, in war and in marriage. By 1721 he owned this plantation on John's Island, besides the Stono, where in 1730, it has been stated, he replaced a log-house with the central portion of Fenwick Hall. Edward Fenwick, son and heir to John, continued in prosperity and about 1750 seems to have placed on each side of the house two-storied brick flankers. The northern one of these now standing, and appropriately used for a garage, was made for a coach-house and coach-horse stable; the one to the south (now completely disappeared) for the stabling of the string of thoroughbreds which Fenwick's numerous importations soon made the most celebrated of their time in the Province, if not in all America. Those who are interested in this stud and lucky enough to be able to get at the book may read its story and that of the Fenwicks in the late Fairfax Harrison's privately printed "John's Island Stud."

In 1787 as the result of a family lawsuit the second Edward Fenwick to own the Hall sold it to his cousin and neighbor, John Gibbes. Shortly after that time, Gibbes probably added the northern wing with its then very fashionable octagonal ends and replaced a simpler entrance with a small portico. As a comment on building methods, it is notable that in this wing the more delicate woodwork is all of white pine, while the heavier panels, carvings and mouldings of the Fenwick building are of Low Country cypress.

Romances have battened to an extraordinary extent on the hot-blooded tribe that held this house for half a century. The Fenwicks gave food for legend, but fancy has outrun fact, both with them and their buildings. Typical of this overgrowth is the legend of an underground passage (almost as common an attribution to any Low Country house as a ghost) that led, according to the stories, from the deep English basement of Fenwick Hall down to the Stono. It was, of course, designed for the escape, possibly necessary, of any desperate character and, in its more ambitious versions, was designed so lavishly that a boat could be hidden in its river end. In fact, however, all this dwindled pitifully to the proportions of a serviceably large drain, through which a not too large boy might creep without great discomfort to dislodge the carcass of a cat.

When the early photograph was made the interior of this house was in a state of seemingly hopeless ruin. Shortly afterwards it was purchased and splendidly restored by Mr. and Mrs. Victor Morawetz, of New York. This house is now the property and residence of Mr. and Mrs. Claude W. Blanchard.

FAIRFIELD
c. 1730

Fairfield Plantation house overlooks the once rich rice fields of the Santee Delta from the first bluff to be found as you go up the river. The tradition that it is the oldest house in that neighborhood is borne out in part by its plan, which is like that of Hampton, and in part by the hard-burned small brick of its high basement, the same sort that was used at Brick House on Edisto Island. Fairfield is one of the first examples of the big wooden plantation houses which thereafter were to be so popular throughout the Low Country.

So far as can be ascertained the oldest part of Fairfield was built by the Lynches, whose home-place, Peachtree, lay next to it on the river. When it belonged to Jacob Motte and his wife Rebecca Brewton Motte, shortly after their marriage in 1758, it consisted of four rooms on its principal floor and two above those on the river side. The Mottes squared out this building by adding two more rooms to the second floor and generally rearranging the interiors, so that windows have been most curiously left, showing on the outside but ceiled over within. The inscription, *Jan. 27, 1766 —Compleated*, scratched into the mortar of one of the chimneys rebuilt to go with this change, would seem to date it.

Fairfield passed from the Mottes to the Pinckneys by the marriage of Elizabeth, daughter of Jacob and Rebecca, to the celebrated Thomas Pinckney in 1779.

After the Revolution, and the death of Elizabeth, Thomas married her sister Frances and surrendered Fairfield to his son and namesake. This Thomas Pinckney probably added the porches—one facing the river, one the land approach—and the small wings that extend the two rooms on the land side. Some time towards the end of the last century Captain Thomas Pinckney, late Confederate States Army, built the little bay windows to the land side of the house.

Fairfield is the property of descendants of Captain Thomas Pinckney.

HAMPTON
1735

About 1735 Noë Serré, grandson and namesake of a Huguenot emigrant, built a substantial plantation house on Wambaw Creek in the settlement of his people known as French Santee. This house formed a part of the fortune of "near £5000 sterling" of his daughter Judith when, in 1757, she married Daniel Huger Horry, member of another prospering Huguenot family. Judith and her two children having died, Horry married again, and profitably, in 1768, Harriott, daughter of Chief Justice Charles Pinckney.

When Horry got it, Hampton, like Fairfield, consisted of four rooms below and two above. Horry now squared out the second story with another pair of rooms and added capacious extensions at either end of it. One of these is taken up completely with the ballroom, floored with single planks of yellow pine running unbroken throughout its length, walled with wide cypress panels, warmed by a huge fireplace that is lined with pictured tiles, and finished at top with a deep-coved ceiling that runs up to the garret floor joists. The front part of the other extension is given up to a great chamber that runs half-way through the second story. Outside of these tall rooms, for the sake of symmetry false windows have been used to line up with those of the second story.

In 1790, in the flush of recovery from the Revolution, the Horrys celebrated the coming of age of the only son, of whom we will hear further at Harrietta, by spreading the deep, and wide, portico completely across the face of Serre's part of the house. It was finished in time for Washington's reception, when he came to breakfast here on his presidential tour.

It may be noted that the portico of Garrick's Thames-side villa, by Robert Adam, is the prototype of this at Hampton. This would make it the first identifiable attempt at the famous Adam style now to be found in South Carolina, where it was to become very popular ten years later. The connection illustrates a family anecdote. Mrs. Charles Pinckney, the Eliza Lucas of indigo fame, who was the grandmother to the Horry heir, was so fond of Garrick's acting that, during a six-year stay in England in the seventeen fifties, she says she "never missed a play where Garrick was to act." It is conjectural that Hampton may have gotten its name from Garrick's Hampton.

It is noteworthy too that this rather large house, which reached its final proportions only after repeated additions, should have attained such a remarkable unity. The variations in the style of the various parts seem merely to parallel in organic growth the history of the families which created it.

Without the house, it is interesting to remark the false windows on the blanked upper walls of the tall ballroom and chamber. Within it, a number of rooms still have fine wall papering in patterns of architectural fantasies and simulated draperies.

From the windows of the great chamber there were primitive slat blinds, notable for the reason that most plantation houses continued the use of solid shutters long after blinds had been used in town.

From the Horrys, Hampton has descended to the sympathetic ownership of Dr. Archibald Rutledge, well-known author, who has made this house, the plantation and the country about it the scene of so much of his work and who has lately made many restorations to his old home.

DRAYTON HALL
1738

In 1738 the Honorable John Drayton, one of His Majesty's Council, bought the land on the Ashley where this house stands. He must at once have started with its building, for his celebrated son, William Henry Drayton, later to be the state's Revolutionary Chief Justice, was born in it in 1742.

The Palladian manner of this big villa is most distinctly appropriate to the time, the place and the builder. Drayton was of the third generation of a Barbadian family come into the colony in 1679 and set up on Ashley River (at Magnolia) about 1700. With the rise of the Province under the Crown the Draytons had become one of a clique of merchant-planter-politician families who were making and marrying themselves into being a sort of Venetian aristocracy. Later the sons of this company hoped, through the Revolution, to set up their own Council of Ten and, freed from English placemen, govern South Carolina even more completely than had their fathers. But in the mid-eighteenth century, the heyday of their prosperity, the latter were fairly satisfied to make Ashley River into a Low Country Brenta, lining its banks with show places, the "palaces" and gardens of a rivalling but related tribe.

Within, Drayton Hall has kept astonishingly well the heavy splendor of detail. About 1800 two old mantels were removed to make place for others in the fashionable style of the brothers Adam. But even then the Draytons of the time had the judgment to leave alone in the lower of the two great halls one whose overmantel is a free adaptation of an illustration in Kent's "Designs of Inigo Jones."

Outside, the house has not been so lucky. In the lawn to the land side can be traced the foundations of two supporting flankers which must have added considerably to the magnificence of the place. On the river side are the still discernible earthworks of a garden which the Duc de la Rochefoucauld-Liancourt preferred to those of Middleton Place.

In 1865, when Sherman's advance through the center of South Carolina forced the evacuation of Charleston, this Ashley River country was left open to the unresisted invasion of a body of Negro troops, somewhat fanatically officered by white men. Of the three houses they left on this river, Drayton Hall is now the sole survivor, saved at the time of the invasion by its owner, a physician, who had the wit to make it terrible by turning it into a hospital for Negroes sick with a virulent form of small-pox.

Drayton Hall is the property of the Draytons of South Carolina.

COMINGTEE
1738

John Coming was the mate of the pioneer ship *Carolina*, among whose passengers was Mistress Affra Harleston. The pair were married in the colony and had grants of land on White Point, and at the T, or Tee, formed where the Eastern and Western Branches of the Cooper River flow together. Coming died childless and his wife left their properties on the river between his nephew, Elias Ball out of Devonshire, and hers, John Harleston, from Ireland. Starting at the focal T, Balls and Harlestons spread their ramifications and plantations until before 1860 they had made the river and its branches a sort of aqueous family tree of their tribes.

In 1738 Elias Ball, the first (there is now a fourteenth), built a substantial brick house across the end of an older wooden one. The last has long since disappeared, but the brick house, though most injudiciously "restored" thirty-odd years ago, still keeps the handsome woodwork the first Ball placed in it, of which the chimney piece with its heavy mouldings is a sample.

Though it would seem obvious enough that the name of this plantation had come from a combination of Coming's and the T in the river, there is an interesting bit of evidence that it was debased from the name of Combe-in-Tene, a village in Coming's native Devonshire.

This house is now the property of the West Virginia Pulp and Paper Company.

OAKLAND
1740

This interesting small house was built on a plantation on the ocean side of Christ Church Parish, probably by Captain George Benison, and about 1740. The house has a rather curious plan. The fireplace, for the sake of giving a large room and still keeping its chimney close to the line of the roof-peak, has been projected pleasantly but oddly from a corner. As at Middleburg, there is a plaster panel above the mantel laid directly upon the brick of the chimney breast.

The kitchen with a couple of other offices and an unusual planting of live oaks form a sort of court at the land front of the house. The distorted chimney is accounted for by its fireplace, made wide enough to burn full-length sticks of cord wood, with a brick oven attached to one side.

Oakland is now the residence of Mr. and Mrs. Ferdinand Gregorie.

TOM SEABROOK'S HOUSE
1740

The Seabrooks are a large and widely-spread Sea-Island family, and somewhat partial to the name of Thomas, so it has been impossible for this writer to determine which of them left his name upon this little Edisto Island plantation house. As its interiors have been radically changed from time to time, dating by its decoration seems also an impossibility, but as these "Dutch" roofs were popular throughout the Low Country about 1740, that would seem a fair year to give to this example.

The house was a vivid case of the way piazzas, if not checked, completely overran Low Country houses in the nineteenth century. This house has been burned down.

PRINCE WILLIAM'S CHURCH, SHELDON 1753

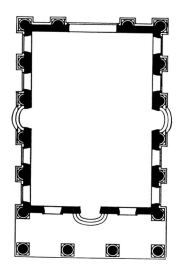

Time has rather justly eclipsed the official title of this church. The name of Prince William's Parish was a loyal compliment to the Royal Duke of Cumberland (he of Culloden). The present name came from the nearby plantation of the Bulls of South Carolina, descendants of the Bulls of Sheldon Hall and Parish in Warwickshire, a family who from the landing of the ship *Carolina* at the first Charles-Town served church and state diligently in the Low Country. Both the provincial Lieutenant Governors Bull aided in the setting up of this parish and the building of the church. Stephen Bull of Sheldon Plantation long ranked peculiarly as its patron, even to the extent of entertaining most of its far-drawn congregation at Sunday dinners, when they mustered from sixty to seventy carriages of various descriptions.

Hoospa Neck, covered by this parish, was part of the rich land lost by the Yemassee Indians after their uprising in 1715. By 1745 it had become thickly enough settled in plantations to warrant its establishment into a parish separate from St. Helena's, and its planters had the wealth to build the most impressive church in the Province outside of Charles-Town.

Unfortunately Sheldon stood in the way of the British force that nearly took Charles-Town, in 1779, and did take vengeance on the country as it returned to Florida. Part of this was the burning of Sheldon. In 1826 the walls were rebuilt upon, but in such uninspired fashion that an ugly church was made from what had been a beautiful ruin. Sherman's 15th Corps, which, as he stated, did "their work up pretty well" going this way in 1865, remedied the mistake of 1826 and left us something beautiful and pathetic.

The date of Sheldon's completion is set up in glazed headers in the chancel wall. The missing brick in the walls are those of the put-log, or put-lock, holes, left open to hold ends of scaffolding and filled up after the job was done.

The John Bull whose handsome tomb with its canting arms and debonairly pious motto is also shown in the drawing had a first wife, a victim of the Yemassee War, who is simply remembered on the family tree as "carried off by the Indians, 1715."

MIDDLETON PLACE 1755

The looting and complete burning of the three residential buildings at Middleton Place by Federal troops in 1865 have left little positive information about the early history of this plantation, and this premier garden of the Thirteen Colonies.

So far as can be determined, this site overlooking the splendid prospect of the Ashley has been kept by one family connection under various names since it was taken from the forests and the Indians in the seventeenth century.

John Williams may be credited for what became the central building, which was probably placed here to command the axis of the great river reach, about 1735. Mary Williams, his only child, married in 1741 Henry Middleton, son of Arthur Middleton, the President of the Council, and brother to the owner of Crowfield. Already of independent fortune, marriage and management would make the first Middleton of Middleton Place one of the province's richest men, who at one time owned fifty thousand acres of land, twenty settled plantations, and about eight hundred Negroes.

That he brought the gardens into being about 1755 is evidenced by two records, and a number of inferences.

The decade after his marriage was peculiarly hard on South Carolina, but the next made up for it. Out of the war years and the temporary loss of the rice market in southern Europe, had come the introduction of indigo. Publicly and privately the province expanded as it had never done before. Charles-Town, with a new outfitting of fine Palladian public buildings, earned the nickname of the Lima of North America. And at the time Henry Middleton had a number of incentives for enriching the handsomest of his plantations. Certainly the remaining flanker, now used as a residence, was built by him in 1755, and carefully marked with his initials and the date. There can be little doubt that this, and its fellow flanker, were integral parts of the garden's design.

The older house, however substantial, is known to have been neither capacious nor excellent. In the time of Arthur Middleton, he would have let it burn, when it accidently caught fire, as a good excuse to be rid of it. In 1755 he was the eldest of five living children, and there would be three more.

There can be every creditable reason for thinking that Henry Middleton wished to surpass his elder brother's great garden, on this far more spectacular site. And in 1754, William Middleton, by selling Crowfield and removing permanently to England, had left Henry chief of the South Carolina branch of the family, with a right to according ostentation.

With a proper plan and supervision, the work was less difficult than would seem. Many of Middleton's plantations made rice, so that his Negroes were trained in banking and ditching. Between crops there was always an idle time. Then gangs could have been brought here to shape terraces, and dig canals, without any interference with plantation work.

A gardener of parts must have had charge of such work. And in 1757 we find a notice from Henry Middleton in the *Gazette* of May 12, to the creditors of his late gardener, George Newman, requesting their accounts. This is all we know of Newman, but until a better claimant is brought forward, we should be allowed to credit him with the bold shaping of the irregular bluff before the houses, the clever changes of axis through the sunken garden, the many-spoked rose garden beyond it, and the gracious proportions of the long canal that separates the planting from the woodlands. Even the great Le Notre must have approved works so much in the spirit of his own.

In 1868, Williams Middleton rebuilt upon the walls of the south flanker, and placed his initials and the date beside those of his great-grandfather. When the west wing was added to this building has not been determined. The baroque gables are obvious, but proper, restorations.

Middleton Place has never left the family that created it. In the present generation Mr. and Mrs. J. J. Pringle Smith splendidly reconditioned the garden.

NORTH CHACHAN 1760

Antoine Cordes, Huguenot physician from Languedoc, founded hereabouts, at the end of the seventeenth century, one of the most extensive and notable of the Low Country families. Chachan soon became a Cordes property. On an inland part of it Francis Marion, grandson to Antoine, was born in 1732. Fifty years later he completed his great career as a partisan leader, in a small but bloody engagement with the British, at the nearby Wadboo Barony house.

The picturesque baroque gables of the stable at Chachan and the ruins of the residence point alike to the period about 1760. Chachan was then the property of a likely builder, James Cordes, the well-to-do bachelor son of a prosperous father.

This stable and a coach-house that matched it faced inward on a court before the land side of the residence. Behind it lay a garden and, beyond that, the land fell away into the rice-fields along the Cooper. The house seems to have been worthy of the handsome arrangement.

By 1811 Chachan had become the property of the able, but legendarily eccentric, Francis Cordes, who in that year placed a handsome pair of gateposts at his entrance on the public road, and marked their crowning marble urns with that date and his name.

About the same time he seems to have spread a tall and massive hexastyle portico across the land side of the residence.

Later he enlarged the court by the addition of a pair of narrow, two-story pavilions. These had tall wooden porticos, in the Greek Revival taste, facing in on the space before the house.

A stickler for order, in certain things, Francis Cordes warded in the roads and paths in this court with a number of stone guard-posts, that now do similar duty at Gippy across the river.

Chachan is now a property of Dr. Edward J. Dennis.

BIGGIN CHURCH 1761

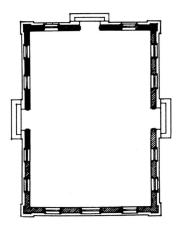

Biggin Hill, in Kent, near London, seems to have sent its name across the ocean to the marl-based hillock crowned by these ruins. The hillock then imposed the name on the swamp-bordered creek at its base, and the Church of St. John's, Berkeley, at its top. The site was donated by the absentee Landgrave John Colleton, from his Wadboo Barony, but it was surely picked by a clerical strategist. For convenience and admonition, it was placed directly in the juncture of three important highways.

The parishioners at the time of the Establishment worshipped in a nearby Huguenot church. Later, when the first Anglican church was constructed, the Huguenots were regularly of its congregation. This burned in 1755, and the building we treat of replaced it in 1761.

The fine situation, that has been greatly changed in the last few years, got the church into trouble in 1781. Nearby Monck's Corner was of considerable tactical importance to the British, who were slowly being bottled up in the neighborhood of Charles-Town. One of their forces, pressed by the Americans, made a stand on Biggin Hill, and used the church as a depot for their stores. When they abandoned these in a night retreat, they set fire impartially to the stores, and the church.

After the Revolution the church was repaired, used, and cared for until the end of the Confederacy. Towards the end of the last century, one of the forest fires, that are a bane to this country, burned the neglected building. For many years its stout walls became a quarry for brick to the locality. Since this book was first undertaken this depredation has been checked, and there have been movements to rebuild Biggin as a place of worship.

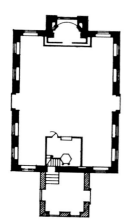

POMPION HILL CHAPEL 1763

Pompion Hill, called "Punkin Hill," is a pleasant run of bluff land with a marsh-free landing on the Eastern Branch of the Cooper River. Here, between 1680 and 1700, a fair-sized community of small plantations grew up, owned mostly by Huguenots. Beyond these were such important places as the Silk Hope Plantation of Governor Sir Nathaniel Johnson and Cacique John Ashby's Quinby Barony.

To serve this community, in 1703 a wooden church, which later became a Chapel of Ease of St. Thomas and St. Denis Parish, was built at Pompion Hill. By 1763 this church was in ruins and its congregation arranged for the building of the one now standing there. The cost, reduced to sterling, was to be £570; the Province allowed £200 of this and the rest was made up by private subscription. Gabriel Manigault, a great Charleston merchant-planter, gave £50 of this amount and, in addition, £10 for 950 red tile that still form cross aisles through the pavement of herring-bone brick.

The considerable care and talent that went into the architecture and construction of the building may be due to the work of Zachariah Villepontoux, whose initials are carved on both sides of the north and south doors. Villepontoux was then a renowned maker of brick at his Parnassus Plantation on Back River and had but lately supplied many used in the building of St. Michael's Church. He was a man of some prominence in his community, a vestryman of Goose Creek, and hardly the person to broadcast his initials in such a way if he only supplied the brick or contracted for its laying. Others who worked with him have also signed the Chapel; William Axson, whom we shall meet again at St. Stephen's, put his name, his insignia as a Freemason and other Masonic emblems on the wall, and there are other, more subordinated, names besides.

As the photograph shows the pulpit end of the Chapel has a floor of wood raised a step above the brick pavements. The ornamental high-backed pews upon it are painted white and were set aside for the white part of the congregation; those of the chancel end, painted a light brown, were used by the Negroes.

Pompion Hill has obviously borrowed the design of its chancel and its pulpit from those of St. Michael's in Charles-Town, then the smart new church of the Province. The pulpit, like much of the woodwork of St. Michael's, is of native red cedar, which from the beginning of the settlement had been a favorite material for cabinet work of various sorts, most particularly for coffins.

The odd, if practical, arrangement of the pulpit and reading desk with regard to the chancel lays a fair task of walking on any minister who completes an Episcopal ritual in this building.

ST. STEPHEN'S CHURCH 1767

The Parish of St. James, Santee, had long been roughly divided into two regions known as French and English Santee, when in 1754 the latter, and upper, part was cut off into St. Stephen's Parish. By then, nearly as French in blood as English, it was full of the prosperity brought by indigo and ready for the chance to show its pride in itself by replacing its decayed wooden chapel with a fine new church.

The Vestry in 1759 agreed with one of their number to make sufficient brick of the size of those of "Mr. Zach Villepontoux's" but rejected them in 1762, and they were not satisfied until a third of their number had made in the third attempt the eminently excellent brick now in the building.

With A. Howard and Francis Villepontoux as supervisors, and tradition says, architects, the work was begun about 1767. Villepontoux, a St. Stephen's man and nephew to Zachariah, with William Axson, who had worked at Pompion Hill, agreed for the brick work and most of the other building operations, as they were let out piecemeal by the Commissioners for the work. Several others, who like Howard and Villepontoux signed the work, completed such smaller operations as the "plaistering" and the stopping of the "putlock holes" before the job was finished in 1769. Axson, however, shows his personal interest in what he did and his zeal as a member of the Wambaw Lodge of Freemasons by neatly inscribing on a couple of ground bricks, set just above the Venetian window of the chancel, his name, his Master Mason's Insignia and representations of the appointments of a Blue Lodge.

Whoever was architect for this church might have profited by Aesop's fable of the frog and the ox, for to finish the ceiling in a style like that of St. Michael's in Charleston the roof has been made too heavy and the chancel window too small for the rest of the design. But any failures the church has in other respects are more than made up for by the virtues of its workmanship, for the same rigorous care went into the laying of the brick as was applied to their burning, and merely the detail of this part of the work is a pleasurable sight.

That a spirit of animated criticism continued throughout the building work is shown by one of the last records concerning it in the Vestry Book—the copy of a letter whereby, objecting strenuously to the "late proceedings in regards to the pewing" of the church, as "somewhat of a very singular nature," Philip Porcher of Oldfield acquaints his fellow commissioners that he will no longer be known as of their number.

ST. JAMES' CHURCH, SANTEE 1768

When in 1706 the country along the south bank of the Santee was made into a parish, the church of the Huguenots, Jamestown, with its name neatly canonized, was appointed the parish church. From that time until the achievement of the present building, this parish projected five other churches and built at least three of them in various parts of its considerable area. At last, when St. Stephen's was cut away from this parish, the present most satisfactory church building was erected, close enough to the bridge across Wambaw Creek to be given sometimes the name of Wambaw Church.

St. James, Santee, has a good claim to be considered the most graceful of the Low Country's parish churches, and this could only be bettered by the removal of certain unhappy improvements, which, however ancient, are still unfortunate. Thus, to form a vestry, a portico, twin to the one shown in the photograph, has been barbarously stopped up with brick walls thrust in between its handsome columns; and within the church the chancel has been reoriented, or rather disoriented, from the east to the north side, where it stops up what was an aisle, loses the long axis that gave it dignity, and has abandoned a charming little Venetian, or Palladian, window designed to back its communion table.

The capitals and bases of the columns of the porticoes appear to be made of ground brick, the body of the columns of brick cast to a curve.

LEWISFIELD 1774

In 1767 Sedgwick Lewis of Cooper River bought a portion of the Fairlawn Barony called Little Landing. With this plantation he dowered his daughter Sarah when, in 1774, she married Keating Simons, grandson of the Huguenot builder of Middleburg. Within a stone's throw of the landing whence the place got its name the Simons built themselves this house, which is in most ways a norm of the plantation houses of the Low Country.

For dryness and airiness the living portion of the house is of frame construction, set high above the ground, on a story built of brick. It is set up foursquare and ample to accommodate the prolific families of those times. The plan is like that of Mulberry, but expanded in most of its dimensions, particularly in those of its bedrooms. And the ceiling even in the second story is set high enough to make sure that on the hottest summer nights there would be plenty of room for any stir of air; for at that time malaria did not drive the plantation people away from their places for all the summer, as it would later when the river swamps were made into rice fields, and besides, building for the hot weather was by then a fixed Low Country obsession. The principal rooms of the house are shaded by a piazza, which also gives a place to sit and taste the coolness coming up from the river, and this is connected with the ground by a broad flight of brick stairs whose ramps flare outward as they descend and end solid cylindrical newels, after the fashion of building in the West Indies. In fact, the architectural pedigree of the house would seem to be a combination of West Indian contrivance with European tradition, adapted to Low Country necessity and materials.

Directly in front of Lewisfield House, Colonel Wade Hampton, during the Revolution, surprised a British force, took seventy-eight prisoners and burned several boats loaded with supplies and plunder. This action also caused Keating Simons, then a paroled prisoner-of-war, to go off and fight with a "rope around his neck," under Marion, whose brigade major he later became.

Lewisfield is now the property of the Hon. Rembert C. Dennis.

REPUBLICAN PERIOD

O TRANTO
1790   The fine hill-site on Goose Creek occupied by this house was used as his place of dwelling by Arthur Middleton, a Barbadian emigrant, who had here a plantation called Yeshoe. Some time before the Revolution the land passed to Dr. Alexander Garden, one of South Carolina's early botanists, a correspondent of the great Linnaeus, who named in his honor the Gardenia that now grows so plentifully throughout the Low Country.

From the Doctor it passed to his son and namesake, Major Garden, once of Light Horse Harry Lee's Legion and author of two books of valuable Revolutionary reminiscences. According to land records and the evidence given by the old decoration of this house itself Major Garden must have been its builder, about 1790.

Otranto long persisted as an active plantation because of the tidal rice fields it had on Goose Creek. But these Goose Creek places, because of their proximity to Charleston, were often used as shooting-boxes, convenient houses for marooning or convivial parties, and after the Confederate War Otranto became the home of a hunting club that still owns it.

A few years ago the house was completely burned out, but it has been restored very nearly to its former state and is the property of the Otranto Club.

T HE BLUFF
1790   Major Isaac Child Harleston, member of a great tribe of Cooper River people, and a man who saw action all through the Cooper River country during the Revolution, seems to have built this little house at his Bluff Plantation on the Western Branch of the river shortly after the war.

Harleston's principal residence was at Irishtown Plantation on the Eastern Branch of the river; and this house on the Western Branch was a subsidiary one. Hence the simplicity, which gives it, however, all the charm that comes with a close attention to the functional needs of a region.

The Bluff is now the plantation home of Mrs. A. F. Storm.

H ARRIETTA
1797   This house, though built in 1797, was never lived in until 1858 because as each heir came of age some unforeseen circumstance prevented his making it his home. Mrs. Horry of Hampton built it as a neighboring place for her daughter Harriott, who in 1797

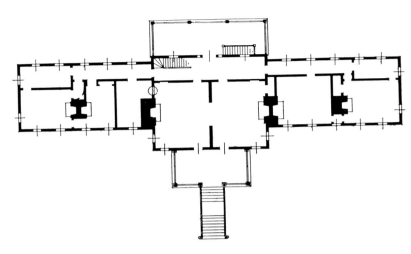

married Frederick Rutledge. But work at Harrietta was stopped when the only son of the Horry family, who had changed his name from Daniel to Charles Lucas Pinckney Horry and had married Elenore Marie Florimonde de Fay la Tour Maubourg, a niece of Lafayette's, decided to make his residence in France. So the Rutledges lived on at Hampton and at last came to own it.

About 1828 work was done to the interiors of the house at the time of the death of C. L. P. Horry and the marriage of the Rutledges' second son, another Frederick, for whom Harrietta was now intended, but the naval career of an older brother left Hampton as a home for this second Frederick and Harrietta remained uninhabited until in 1858 it came into the possession of Stephen D. Doar, who repaired it, and at last the house was lived in.

Three generations of his family had owned Harrietta when the heirs of David Doar sold it in 1930, and even then there were rooms in the ample house that had never been plastered!

When Horatio and Sophie Meldrim Shonnard made Harrietta their winter home in 1930, Hendrick Wallin, of Savannah, reconditioned the house. He very handsomely, and appropriately, added the fine entrance stairs at what had been the rear, and gave the interior its first respectable stairway, in place of the very meager one shown in our plan. At the same time the grounds, with their fine plantings of old camellias, were landscaped by Humberto Innocenti.

Recently Harrietta has belonged to the Abney family connection.

The house possesses an amusing bit of architectural trickery. Because of the careful balancing of windows and doors in the principal rooms, two doors were thrown into disagreeable closeness to each other, under the portico on the garden side. To avoid such effects as resulted at Lawson's Pond and Springfield, a false door was inserted between the two at Harrietta and the three were framed in with a common order. The segmental window in the pediment of the garden portico is also a false contrivance for the sake of looks. There is too an interesting dumb waiter; it is built to look like a door, whose upper portion, fitted with shelves and swung on a vertical pivot, carries dishes from the pantry to the dining room.

Harrietta is placed as a rice planter's house should be, with a direct outlook over its fields.

El Dorado
1797

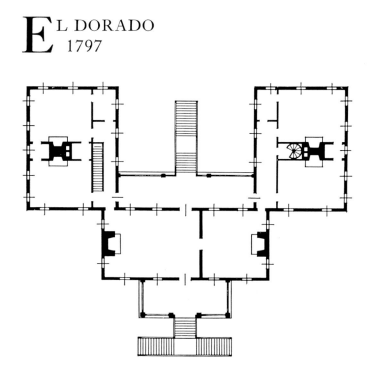

El Dorado came out of the prosperity that followed the spread of tidal rice culture. At that time Rebecca Motte sold the Congaree plantation made famous as Fort Motte, where she had instigated the firing of her house to dislodge the British force garrisoning it. Here, near to Fairfield where we have already made note of her, she began this fine plantation.

On his return from his successful mission to treat with Spain, Thomas Pinckney married his deceased wife's sister, Frances Motte, widow of John Middleton of Crowfield. With her and with her mother, Pinckney did a considerable amount of building, using his own trained workmen. It was at the same time that he was working on his stepson's estate to build the big mansion on George Street in Charleston, that he appears to have worked with Mrs. Motte on the house at El Dorado.

The plan illustrated here was taken from the ruins of the house, most unfortunately burned about a hundred years after its building. Details were supplied for this resoration by members of the family who had lived in El Dorado. Old photographs show the house to have had a portico on the river front similar to those at Fairfield and the one on the garden side of Harrietta built by Thomas Pinckney's sister, Mrs. Horry. Similar plans were used for the plantation house of the Gibbes' at Rose Hill on the Combahee, of which there is a painting in the Charleston Museum, and for the tabby plantation house of the Sams family on Dawtaw Island, near Beaufort, now in ruins. As developed at El Dorado, the plan offers an interesting contrast to the scheme of Harrietta, where the same search for pleasant exposures to the rooms has been resolved in a different manner.

The Spanish name of the plantation, reminiscent of Thomas Pinckney's diplomatic work just before its settlement, was suggested by the golden flower of the pitcher plant that abounded there.

The late Josephine Pinckney, then owner of El Dorado, assisted vitally, here and elsewhere, in the preparations for this book.

BELVIDERE
1800

Towards the end of the Proprietorial Era this property became the site of the "Governor's House," an official residence of English governors of the Province. At the end of the eighteenth century, while it belonged to Colonel Thomas Shubrick, the old residence was burned. The Shubricks replaced it with this very fine example of the Low Country's version of Adam style.

The place at that time was like several about it on the "Neck," a cross between plantation and suburban farm, the house close enough to Charleston to serve as a town residence, and its decoration correspondingly elaborate. The plainness of the entrance face may be accounted for by a long-vanished portico. The flankers on the river side were among the last left in the Low Country.

For many years Belvidere handsomely housed the Charleston Country Club and its fields sloping down to the Cooper furnished a golf course. The house has been destroyed.

LOWNDES' GROVE
1803

This former suburban residence stands directly across the Ashley from the little point where Charleston was begun in 1670. The name of the Grove, now taken by the street this house uses, came from an older property, a half mile inland. Here, before the Revolution, John Gibbes had a house, which he had surrounded with a large and very handsome garden, equipped with pineries and greenhouses. The British force that came near capturing Charles Town in 1779 burned the house and caused the death of its owner in a fury of chagrin. The gardens remained to be shown in some detail on Sir Henry Clinton's map for the siege of 1780, and to excite the very considerable admiration of the Hessians, who were quartered near it.

In 1803 the part of Gibbes' property carrying the old name was bought by William Lowndes, who had just married a daughter of Thomas Pinckney and who evidently proceeded to build himself this home. Lowndes became later the most distinguished member of his long well-known family. He was of the group of congressmen and senators from South Carolina who, from their sheer brilliance, took over the leadership of the South from Virginia at the time of the War of 1812. He was a shining example of the Low Country planter in politics—one of the nearest approximations in American public life to the able, independent, country-gentlemen members of the English Parliament.

For a number of years Albert Gallatin and Ruth Hanna MacCormick Simms, who, like the builder of this house, had been prominent in national service, made their winter home here.

The Grove is now the residence of Mr. and Mrs. Walter K. Prause.

THE ROCKS
1805

Captain Peter Gaillard when nearly ruined by the failure of indigo bought this plantation to make food for his people, about 1797, and proceeded to make a fortune planting cotton upon it.

In the plantation book he started with The Rocks, and in which he kept the birthdays of his children and his Negroes, the accounts of his wines and those of his long-continued experiments in cotton culture, he records the building of this house. The first item concerning it is entered on May 11, 1803, when he writes, "Began this day to saw Cypress & get shingles for the Rocks." He reports at the same time items about a pipe of wine. On Septr. 1, he begins to make brick. On October 12, a carpenter, a Mr. Bowles, begins work making sash. Two other carpenters are engaged, one in November, the other in December, and Negro artisans from other plantations shortly begin to appear and disappear, as do also sundry cases of rum for the white carpenters and demijohns of the same liquor for the colored ones. Feb. 22, 1804, the first brick was laid in the foundation of the house. April 4, the cotton planting for the year was finished and between that day and the seventh the house was raised. June 3, Gaillard agrees with his carpenter, Mr. Walker, to have the chimney pieces and doors of the house made that summer at the North and delivered in Charleston at Charleston prices, "Two of the chimney pieces to be done in a genteel but plain style, & five others being for the bed rooms to be very plain." With comings and goings of workmen and rum the work then continues until on April 15, 1805, "Billy the Painter" finished his work and received the last payment made.

The mantel illustrated is one of those specified to be genteel but plain.

The Rocks, using the plan of older houses in the neighborhood, in Upper and Middle St. John's, is followed in its use by many others; essentially it is that of Ophir and of Springfield, without the wings peculiar to the last particular example. The three small windows at the rear of The Rocks give light to the broad stair landing that in some of these houses is in part closed off to make a curious little mezzanine room.

When the old site of this house was to be flooded by the Santee-Cooper Project, its owner, Mr. J. Rutledge Connor, removed the old house to a different part of his property. It is, in 1964, the residence of his son and namesake.

WAPPAOOLA
1806

The older portion of this house was built in 1806 by the Reverend Milward Pogson who, by his marriage with Henrietta Wragg, came into this portion of a great Wragg property. The reverend gentleman is supposed to have made his building

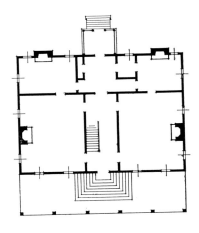

about the frame of a barn he bought already laid out and cut in Charleston, and his in-laws never allowed the country to forget the story.

His agreeable brick-paved porch with its heavy columns is reminiscent of the one at Otranto, where Pogson had lived while he was rector of Goose Creek Church. The wings projecting at the back of the house were added in 1928 when Wappaoola was the property of Mr. Owen Winston and Mr. William Henry Barnum. At the same time its very plain interiors were decorated with old mantels from Charleston and with cornices of contemporary design.

Wappaoola, signifying Sweet Water in an Indian tongue, takes its name from the nearby creek that made it a rich rice plantation. This house has lately made way for a modern dwelling.

MOUNT HOPE
1807

Colonel Lewis Morris, of the Morrisania family and of General Nathanael Greene's staff, and one of a number of officers left in the Low Country by the invasion of that friendly army, married into a plantation. About 1807 he and his wife, who had been Anne Barnett Elliott, built this house on the high bluff overlooking that portion of the Edisto River called the Pon Pon (an Indian name signifying Big Bends), where had once been projected the never quite realized colonial town of Wilton.

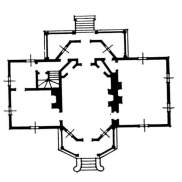

Mount Hope house has a plan that is an interesting plantation adaptation of the fashion of building then very prevalent in Charleston, and to be seen notably in the Nathaniel Russell house and the house built by Thomas Pinckney on George Street. The polygonal room of this plantation house gives an interesting contrast to those at the Grove, lower down the river, built by George Washington Morris, the son of Lewis Morris of Mount Hope.

Mount Hope is now the residence of Mr. and Mrs. Charles Heyward Jervey.

EUTAW
1808

The Sinklers of Old Santee, who had been indigo planters, came into Upper St. John's after the Revolution and established themselves at Belvidere, where they were among the pioneers of cotton planting. William Sinkler, a son of the family at Belvidere, in 1808 built Eutaw across the clear and lovely creek of that name and established there a branch of the family.

The interesting little building in the yard at Eutaw, bearing a far-off resemblance to the *Maison Carrée* at Nîmes, and known as the Lodge, was originally designed to be the office of a doctor-planter member of the family connection.

Our photograph of the parlor shows, on the mantel, a silver pitcher taken by "Janet Berkeley", one of the family thoroughbreds, at the Pineville races. The Sinklers were always keen horsemen, and Eutaw was famous, not only for its stud, but, in William Sinkler's time, for a great Negro trainer, Hercules, or Old Hark, who had a reputation all over the state for his ability and judgment.

Part of the arched piazza foundations of Eutaw house was made of brick got from the ruins of the house the British made the center of their line in the crucial battle of Eutaw Springs.

After having been throughout its existence a home of the family that built it, the Eutaw house was torn down to make way for the Santee-Cooper Project.

MARSHLANDS 1810

The Marshlands house, which was for years included in the Navy Yard, was built by John Ball, a great Cooper River rice planter, soon after he bought a plantation here in 1810.

The lavish and excellently executed gouge work used at Marshlands to supplement its more formal Adam enrichments may have been forced on its builder by the embargoes and other interruptions to trade with England, whence the Adam ornaments came. Later, American putty workers substituted patriotic eagles for the lost nymphs, and stars for the classic rosettes, but gouge work, particularly among these plantations, had by then pretty well taken the place of the older style.

This work at Marshlands was similar to that in the town house of John Ball's father and was probably by the same hand. The interiors of the older Ball's house are now in the home of Ellery Sedgwick, in Massachusetts, and are in part illustrated in the "Georgian Period."

In 1961 the College of Charleston removed this house to its property at Fort Johnson, where it will be restored.

OPHIR 1810

Ophir, with Mexico, was one of the three plantations of Peter Porcher, of Peru, who believed in giving his places the names of famous gold-mines and in attempting by strenuous management to make them live up to their namesakes' reputations. Ophir Plantation house appears to have been built by Colonel Thomas Porcher, son of Peter, in or about 1810. The floor plan of this house is typical more of Upper than of Middle St. John's where Ophir stands, as in everything but exact proportion it is almost a replica of that used by Porcher's brother-in-law Peter Gaillard at The Rocks.

It is interesting to note the varied use of the same motifs on this exterior cornice at Ophir and on that of the parlor at The Rocks.

Ophir remained Porcher property until destroyed in the construction of the Santee-Cooper Project.

WILLIAM SEABROOK'S HOUSE 1810

Not long after 1810 William Seabrook, one of the first planters who had realized a fortune from the culture of Sea Island cotton, built this house and signed it with his initials in the iron work on the entrance stair.

His house is now the most ornate of those left on Edisto Island from the early Republican days. It is interesting to see how the portico in two stories, long popular in Charleston and the Low Country, has been restated on this house, with the flat arches then so frequently used on the piazzas in the town used here in the upper story.

The plan of this house became the classic one on Edisto from this time forward. With variations in the arrangement of the stair it is repeated in the '20's at Oak Island, the home of Seabrook's son, and in the '40's at Peter's Point, on the other side of the

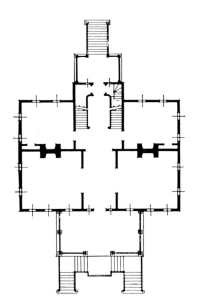

island. Only in each instance, with the natural changes in style, the ceilings of the rooms are progressively heightened and the ornament is more suppressed.

William Seabrook's House has been ascribed by tradition to Hoban, architect of the White House, who practised in Charleston for a short time during the 1790's but nothing has been found to confirm this story, nor is there known now any local work of Hoban's which would serve as a comparison.

The Federal capture of Port Royal in the first autumn of the Confederate War forced General Robert E. Lee, then in command of South Carolina and Georgia, to transfer his coast defences within the line of the Sea Islands and withdraw their people. Such houses as this were often left all but fully furnished, standing in a No-Man's-Land, hunted over for stray cattle and hogs by foraging parties and scouts from the Federal Navy and the Confederate Army. Later in the Federal advance along the Sea Islands towards Charleston this house was occupied by various military units both as staff headquarters and as provost. Idling soldiers and prisoners have covered the walls of the attic with names, rosters of regiments and boasts of future revenge against Charleston, and have sketched on the white plaster, sometimes with considerable vividness, soldiers, cannon and patriotic emblems.

When the war ended the Negroes crowded to these islands, promised them by Sherman's famous confiscating order. Houses like this became communal dwellings, a family in each room, and the dining room a church and meeting hall, with sometimes the sideboard for a pulpit. Later, after their owners had recovered them, many fell vacant, as did this house, too large to keep up, even to keep warm, in less prosperous days. It may have been when William Seabrook's mansion was lying grim, cold and vacant, that someone added to the hot inscriptions on its walls the words: *Dum tacet clamant.*

Since the photographs were made this house has been very thoroughly reconditioned by its present owner, Mr. Donald D. Dodge of Philadelphia.

THE ELMS
1810

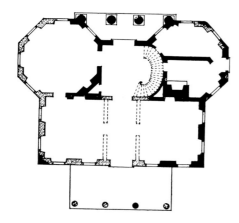

The Izards were one of the first great Goose Creek families who had much to do with setting the pattern of life in the Low Country. Their first house at this plantation was finished about the same time as the Church of St. James', where this family worshipped and were buried. The style of the residence, from what meager descriptions remain, seems to have been quite like that of the church, with scutcheons and other such ornaments in stucco. Ralph Izard, its most celebrated owner, in condemning them to destruction, called them "plaster-headed house-hold Gods," but they seem to have survived his time.

He was one of the notable South Carolina Nabobs who lived abroad for years before the Revolution. In 1774 he and his wife, the former Alice De Lancey, of New York, sat to Copley for the famous conversation piece he painted of them in Rome. So the pair may now be seen in the Boston Museum of Fine Arts, seated very elegantly at table, attended by antique statues, and a distant view of the Colosseum.

About 1809 the old house, with or without its enrichments of stucco, was destroyed by fire. Henry Izard replaced it with the very interesting building we show. The Elms passed out of the Izards' possession after his death.

Following the damages of the earthquake of 1886, the house was allowed to fall into decay. For many years its ruins have been a most spectacular architectural ghost. Surrounded by jungle, you came in sight of them only when they were looming over you.   Part of their breath-taking effect was lost when laborious vandals over-threw the two great white columns that once showed bravely over the rice-fields of Goose Creek.

The Elms is owned by the Commissioners of Public Works of Charleston.

**SPRINGFIELD
1818**
Joseph Palmer notes in his plantation book, kept at his Springfield Plantation in Upper St. John's: "Mr. Champlin commenced on Monday the 20 October 1817 to build a Dwelling House for me, 46 feet by 40 with a wing at Each End, 22 by 16 feet at Sixty Dollars per month.   Joseph Palmer."

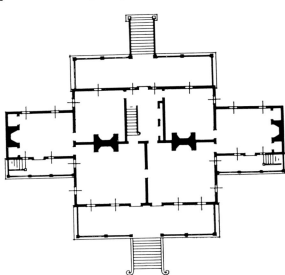

Later, after he had itemized in like fashion the comings in and acquittings of Negro artisans hired from planters in the neighborhood and the occasional comings and goings of Champlin, Palmer notes:

By Seven months & 3 Days work of
George Champlin ending on 17
June 1818 . . . @ $60 . . . $429
By the hire of one of Major S. Porcher's Carpenters . . . @ $20
per month, being with me for the
good of Champlin 140
By Ditto of Mr. Champlin's ap-
prentice Harry 40
                                   _____
                                    $609

And with so much of specification, of drawings, contractings and general arrangings a house was had.

There is unfortunately no note of the carver who worked upon the elaborate door and window frames, the mantels and chimney breasts of this big house—in its way the high point, the very apogee of its ornate style, in the midst of a territory where that style was very popular—for a contrast of the work at Springfield with that at Lawson's Pond and at White Hall shows how a country version of the gouge work at Marshlands spread itself through Upper and Middle St. John's among the second generation of plantation houses in this cotton region. This house remained a home of the Palmers until destroyed in the construction of the Santee-Cooper Project.

**TOMOTLEY
1820**
The spectacular avenue at Tomotley is a brilliant illustration of the fact that, however venerable their appearance, there are but few avenues of live oaks in the Low Country much more than a hundred years old.

Tomotley has a long history. It is a part of the barony granted to Landgrave Edmund Bellinger about Tomotley Savannah, in the Yemassee country, at the beginning of the eighteenth century. In 1755 the name passed with a plantation cut out of the original grant of 13,000 acres to Izards of the Goose Creek family, but it was not until after 1820 that Patience W. B. Izard, wife of Abraham Eustis, and the last Izard owner of Tomotley, beautified Tomotley with a number of avenues that radiate from the site of her house. This planting is an illustration of the strong tendency among the Izards to decorate with fine houses and plantings of gardens and avenues any place where they set themselves down.

In 1964 Tomotley, with its avenues, was the property of Mr. G. H. Bostwick.

WHITE HALL 1822 Thomas Porcher, son of the builder of Ophir, appears to have built the older part of White Hall at the time of his marriage with Catherine Gaillard in 1822. The decoration may well have come from the same hands that did the work at Springfield and Lawson's Pond.

The wing with the bow window and the piazza with the square columns were added to the house in 1854 by Dr. Charles Lucas, husband of Elizabeth Lydia Porcher.

White Hall was the home of the Lucas family until it was destroyed in the construction of the Santee-Cooper Project.

LAWSON'S POND 1823 Charles Cordes Porcher inherited this plantation from his father in 1817. He appears to have built this house in preparation for his marriage with Rebecca Marion in 1823. The twin doors, here, are almost a specialty of Upper St. John's. The considerable similarity of detail and design leads to the belief that this house may have been constructed by the same George Champlin who worked at Springfield for Joseph Palmer.

Lawson's Pond has long been a home of the Couturiers.

THE WEDGE 1826 This plantation gets its name from its peculiar shape, for from a bearing on the big-road that gives barely the space for a couple of gates it widens to a broad expanse of rice fields on the Santee. The Wedge was long owned by William Lucas, son of Jonathan Lucas who in this same neighborhood invented the first successful rice-pounding mill, the mill that did for the grain what Whitney's gin did for the cotton staple.

In 1826 William Lucas built this capacious house, which was owned and inhabited by his family for the following century. It was purchased from the Lucases in 1929 by Mr. and Mrs. Elbridge Gerry Chadwick, who in restoring it have added to and built upon the great charms of the place and its planting.

It is worthy of note that William Lucas should have subordinated the then new Greek Revival style to the vernacular of the country. And if he used columns of wood proportioned like those of a Doric temple, he subdued them to the general scheme of a plantation house, for the Low Country and Charleston can boast that when they borrowed that most reverend style, in anything like its full proportion, they used it only for buildings that were to be reverenced, and hid no private dwelling behind a pseudo-Parthenaic portico, in wood and in little.

The Wedge is now the winter residence of Mr. and Mrs. Charles H. Woodward, of Philadelphia.

D EAN HALL
1827   The Nisbetts of Dean, a family of Scottish baronets, owned Dean Hall for nearly a century before it was bought in 1821 by William Augustus Carson and his mother. Carson, son of a rich Charleston merchant, studied at Harvard, where he was one of a number of South Carolinians who belonged to Porcellian. He then turned to rice planting and developed a passion for the occupation. Dean Hall was under him long celebrated for the splendid order and comfort of its conduct. His house, built in 1827, of brick made just across the Back River at Medway, is a fine example of the planning of a man who knew his country and how best to live in it. From his encompassing piazza he could look over his rice fields, spreading from the foot of the hill where the house is set out towards the "T" of the Cooper River; or out over his upland plantings; or toward his Negro street with its model arrangement. Live oaks do not crowd about the house like so many vegetable Bulls of Bashan cutting off air and light however romantic they may be. But that same piazza supplies the shade to the big rooms trees would have given, and it also supplies a variety of choice in sunshine and shade the year and the house around.

Under the brick arcade are the windows of the service rooms, kitchens, storerooms and the like placed in the flag-paved basement.

Dean Hall in 1909 was sold by James Petigru Carson, son of William Carson, to the late Benjamin R. Kittredge of New York. In the years that have passed the Kittredge family has created on this plantation one of the great gardens of the Low Country. Like all rice plantations on salty rivers Dean Hall had depended for fresh water on "Reserves". These had been made by damming a series of cypress swamps, which thus became a network of mysteriously beautiful lakes. From these have been made the celebrated Cypress Gardens.

THE GROVE
1828

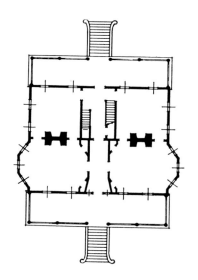

This rice-plantation house was built on the Pon Pon about 1828 by George Washington Morris near his father's house at Mount Hope. The Grove is chiefly notable for its rather unusual use of polygonal rooms and furnishes an interesting contrast in this respect to those at Mount Hope and at The Elms.

After the taking of the photograph used in this book, The Grove underwent a very sympathetic restoration in 1929, upon becoming the property of Mr. Owen Winston.

The polygonal piazza columns used at this house are variations on the style of the Greek Revival worked flat with a plane, as if by a skillful country carpenter, for they show quite a proper sense of proportion. The flight of steps, shown on the plan but not on the photograph, is a part of the recent restoration.

In 1964 the Grove is the home of Mr. and Mrs. R. Carter Henry.

THE LAUNCH
1830

In 1827 Oliver Hering Middleton married a Sea Island heiress. He was a young man with a rather cosmopolitan rearing, a son of Henry Middleton, of Middleton Place, who just at that time was the United States Minister to Russia. His bride was Susan Chisolm the only surviving daughter of Dr. Robert Trail Chisolm. From him she inherited this Edisto plantation called The Launch, probably because of the fine bluff above Governor's Creek, where boats could be put overboard, and where the Middletons apparently built this house, in time to have a daughter born there, in January 1830.

The taste of its unidentified architect becomes the more apparent, the more his work is studied. The fundamentals then in demand are met generously. The rooms provided, if few, are placed well above the soil, are large and high, and have plenty of cross ventilation. But masses and voids have been kept in hand. The triple windows look well on the outside and leave big spaces at the inside of the house. In place of the never too comely piazzas, there is the roomy dignified porch at the front and the loggia-like gallery at the back. This is compassed in by the low wings, and serves not only as a piazza would, but gives free circulation from the wings to the central hallway, other than through the principal rooms.

In our photograph, unfortunately, the proportion of the loggia is hurt by the siding that hides the upper parts of the columns.

Dr. and Mrs. Jenkins Mikell Pope have long made this fine house their home.

PRESBYTERIAN CHURCH, EDISTO
1831

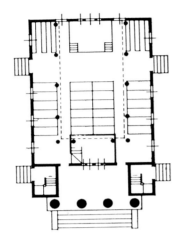

This church serves one of the oldest of the Presbyterian congregations in South Carolina, and outside of Charleston.

In 1830-1831 the congregation had a Mr. Pillans erect this building, to take the place of an older one that had become inadequate. The Edisto Community of Sea Island cotton planters was in such affluent case that the building fund was considerably oversubscribed, and the resultant surplus given as a bonus to the builder.

His work seems not to have been altogether satisfactory, for when William Seabrook, whose house we have noticed, died in 1836, the legacy of $5,000 he left this church was promptly spent on improvements. E. M. Curtis, of Charleston, then replaced a portico of far slimmer dimensions with the fine Greek Doric design we picture. The rest of the bequest went to putting a coved ceiling over the interior.

The arrangement of the church is a direct statement of its function. By then the general revival of religion that had begun in the early 1800's had not only swept back into orthodoxy of the fashionable sorts most of the planter-people but had also brought into the churches large numbers of Negro communicants as well. For these galleries were provided, or set aside, in the churches, and in this church two were especially constructed. Separate admission was given to these galleries through the forward doors on the sides, and by way of stairs housed in the pylons beside the Doric porch. At that time the Presbyterians of this region communed seated at tables spread across the wide spaces provided in front of their churches' tribunes, or pulpits, and at this church pairs of doors were provided at the ends of the table space for the colored communicants, who followed the whites at table and were served in their turn by the white elders of the church.

SOMERTON
1836

Somerton, which like Somerset gets its name from its long-ago connection with the Reverend William Screven, was afterwards the original settlement of the Ravenel family in Middle St. John's, and long a burial place for their far-flung connection.

In 1836, Frederick Adolphus Porcher, later a professor at the College of Charleston and one of the Charleston *literati* of the mid-nineteenth century, built at Somerton the house illustrated.

The house was somewhat notable for the simple delicacy of its detail, particularly shown in the columns of the porch. These were worked to sixteen flat sides and carefully given entasis. Unfortunately, since these photographs were made Somerton house has been completely destroyed by fire.

MAGNOLIA GARDENS 1840

The bluffland whence this very celebrated garden overlooks the Ashley has been a property of the Drayton family, their ancestors and descendants, since about 1700.

In the middle years of the nineteenth century John Grimké, by taking the surname Drayton, under the will of his grandfather, Thomas Drayton, became the owner of Magnolia. John Grimké Drayton was both a planter and an Episcopal clergyman, but a clergyman's sore-throat gradually forced him more and more out of the active ministry. Turning to gardening, he then created one of the most beautiful things in the Low Country.

According to tradition he received the first of the *Azalea indica*, which he made the chief glories of his garden, from relatives in Philadelphia where the plants had been introduced but had not thriven. Before his death he had made at Magnolia one of the most notable collections of this lovely flower in the world. But far more than that he had used the brilliant tones of the azaleas and the rich somber hues of the Low Country woods and waters to paint in his garden a most gorgeous contrasting series of living pictures, veritable works of art.

So celebrated now as hardly to need description, this man's work has continued in the care and possession of his descendants, and Magnolia is now the property of C. Norwood Hastie and J. Drayton Hastie, his great grandsons.

BOONE HALL 1843

Boone Hall was granted at the end of the seventeenth century to Major John Boone, who, with his brother Joseph, was heavily engaged in colonial politics about that time. The plantation was kept by the Boones until shortly before 1817. In that year it was purchased by John and Henry Horlbeck, whose family kept it until a few years ago. These brothers were sons to John Horlbeck of Plauen in Saxony, who, with his brother Peter, came to Charleston in the middle of the eighteenth century and became there eminent architect-builders. They were the constructors of the old Exchange Building at the foot of Broad Street, in Charleston.

John Horlbeck, the first, seems to have transmitted to his posterity both an ability to work in fraternal combinations and a taste for the building business, for his sons and their descendants long held Boone Hall as an undivided family property and, whatever might be their individual concerns, conducted on their plantation a large and thriving brickyard.

In 1842 Henry Horlbeck's eleven children turned over the conduct of Boone Hall to four of their number—John, Henry, Daniel and Edward. Among the early improvements of their ménage, they set out the avenue to the house and marked it with a marble slab stating that it was planted in 1843, and it is reasonable to assume that the substantial line of brick houses with pan-tile roofs, forming the Negro street that runs on the creek side of this avenue, dates from about the same time and was another of the four brothers' works.

The property continued with the Horlbecks until 1935. It was then purchased by the Honorable and Mrs. Thomas A. Stone, of the Canadian Diplomatic Corps. The Stones replaced a simple old wooden house with a handsome new one, built of brick got from the long abandoned Horlbeck brickyard.

In 1964 the plantation was in the possession of the McRae family.

GIPPY
1852

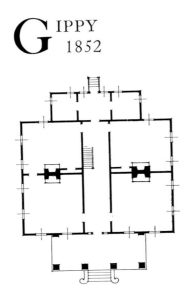

It is an interesting comment on the individualism of Low Country architecture that we should arrive at the end of its last great era before we find a house that would fulfill the popular idea of a Southern colonial mansion. Gippy Plantation, once a part of the Fairlawn Barony, on the Western Branch of the Cooper, was so named after a local swamp, where an old Negro named Gippy, an inveterate runaway, used to hide out in a hollow tree. In 1852 John Sims White lost by fire the house his father had built on this plantation. To help him out all the neighborhood recruited their Negro artisans, and this house was built in record time.

The present owners, Mr. and Mrs. Nicholas G. Roosevelt of Philadelphia, among their additions to the house have altered the porch by giving it round columns in place of square ones. They have also since this photograph was taken very much enlarged the old garden and added to the planting around the house.

Gippy is one of the plantations that has come most actively into a new and useful life. Its rice fields are again in cultivation. Its upland fields are under crops of grain or serving as pasture for great flocks of sheep and a superb herd of Guernsey cattle.

SOMERSET
1852

The Reverend William Screven, an Antipaedobaptist minister and ship carpenter, born in the county town of Somerton in Somersetshire, went thence to Maine, where in Kittery he suffered much for his opinions concerning infant baptism. Thence he came to Charles-Town just at the end of the seventeenth century and purchasing lands in Berkeley County left on them the names Somerset and Somerton.

William Cain, who later became a Lieutenant Governor of South Carolina, bought this plantation in 1827 with the basis of this house upon it. This had probably been built some length of time before by one of the several Mazycks, or Ravenels, who had owned the property. In 1852 the Cains remodelled the house so extensively that everything of architectural significance, shown by our picture, can be counted from that time.

Somerset continued as a home for the Cains of Middle St. John's, Berkeley, until its destruction by the Santee-Cooper Project.

PROSPECT HILL
1878

Prospect Hill, on the Pon Pon or Edisto River, was built by Edward Barnwell to replace his house burned by Federal invaders. In 1964 is was the property of Mr. and Mrs. James S. Rogers.

ILLUSTRATIONS

THE PHOTOGRAPHS WERE TAKEN
BY BEN JUDAH LUBSCHEZ IN 1928
AND BY FRANCES BENJAMIN JOHN-
STON IN 1938. THE ADDITIONAL
PHOTOGRAPHS ARE BY CHARLES
RICHARD BANKS. ALL ARE INDI-
CATED BY THE PHOTOGRAPHERS'
INITIALS.

MEDWAY, 1686, South Side

F. B. J.

MEDWAY, The Double Avenue

F. B. J.

MEDWAY, North Side   F. B. J.

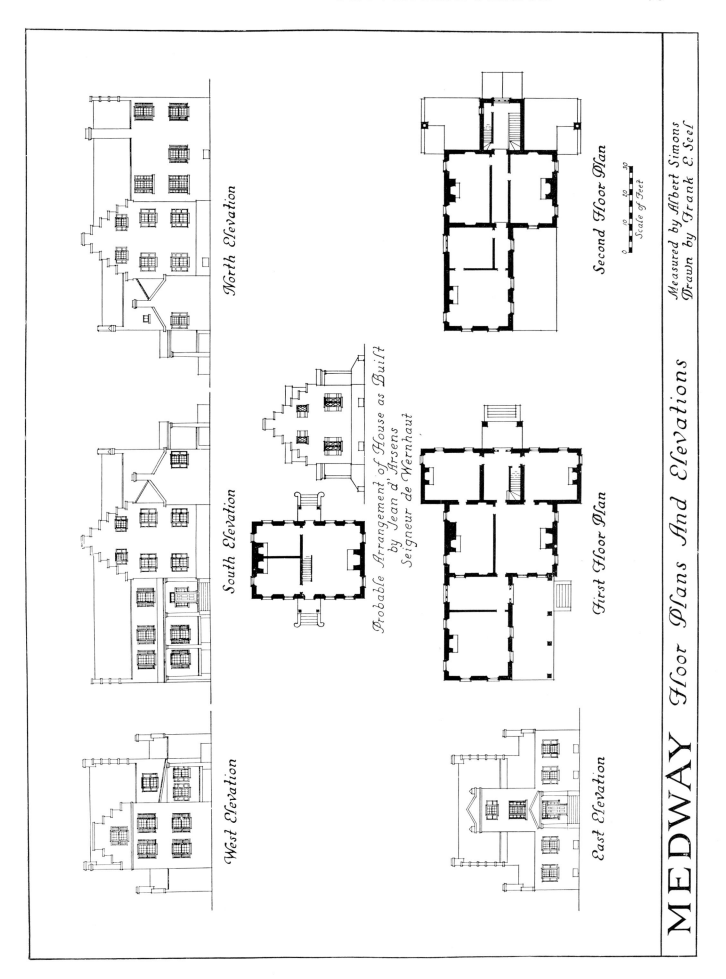

North Elevation

South Elevation

West Elevation

East Elevation

Second Floor Plan

First Floor Plan

Probable Arrangement of House as Built
by Jean d'Arsens
Seigneur de Wernhaut

Scale of Feet

Measured by Albert Simons
Drawn by Frank E. Seel

MEDWAY Floor Plans And Elevations

MIDDLEBURG, 1699   B. J. L.

MIDDLEBURG, Bed Room, Second Floor   B. J. L.

MIDDLEBURG, Drawing Room

B. J. L.

MIDDLEBURG, Kitchen

B. J. L.

MIDDLEBURG, Commissary   F. B. J.

MIDDLEBURG, Stable   B. J. L.

ST. ANDREW'S CHURCH, 1706

F. B. J.

ST. ANDREW'S CHURCH   F. B. J.

ST. ANDREW'S CHURCH

B. J. L.

C. R. B.

ST. JAMES' CHURCH, GOOSE CREEK, 1708

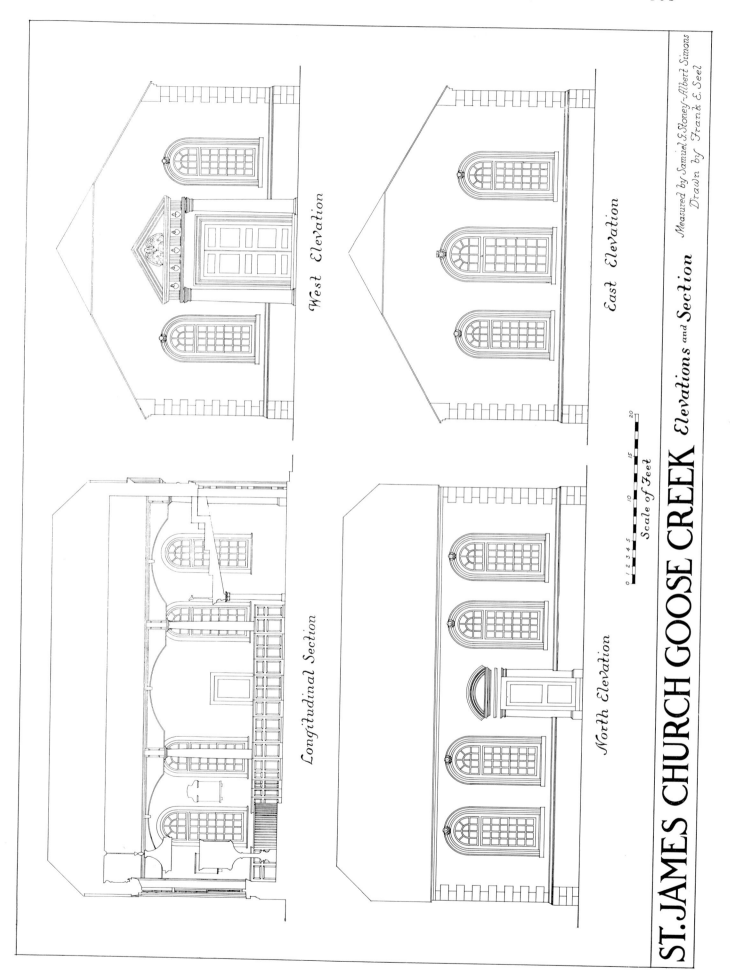

West Elevation

East Elevation

Longitudinal Section

North Elevation

Scale of Feet

ST. JAMES CHURCH GOOSE CREEK Elevations and Section

Measured by Samuel E. Stoney–Albert Simons
Drawn by Frank E. Seel

F. B. J.

ST. JAMES' CHURCH, GOOSE CREEK

ST. JAMES' CHURCH, GOOSE CREEK

F.B.J.

ST. JAMES' CHURCH, GOOSE CREEK   F. B. J.

ST. JAMES CHURCH GOOSE CREEK *Elevation of Chancel*

Measured by Samuel G Stoney–Albert Simons
Drawn by Frank E Seel

Scale of Feet

MULBERRY, 1714   B. J. L.

MULBERRY   F. B. J.

MULBERRY, Rice Field

F. B. J.

MULBERRY

B. J. L.

MULBERRY, Dining Room

B. J. L.

MULBERRY, Drawing Room

B. J. L.

F. B. J.

MULBERRY, Bedroom, Second Floor

HANOVER, 1720, St. John's Berkeley   C. R. B.

HANOVER, 1940, Clemson College   C. R. B.

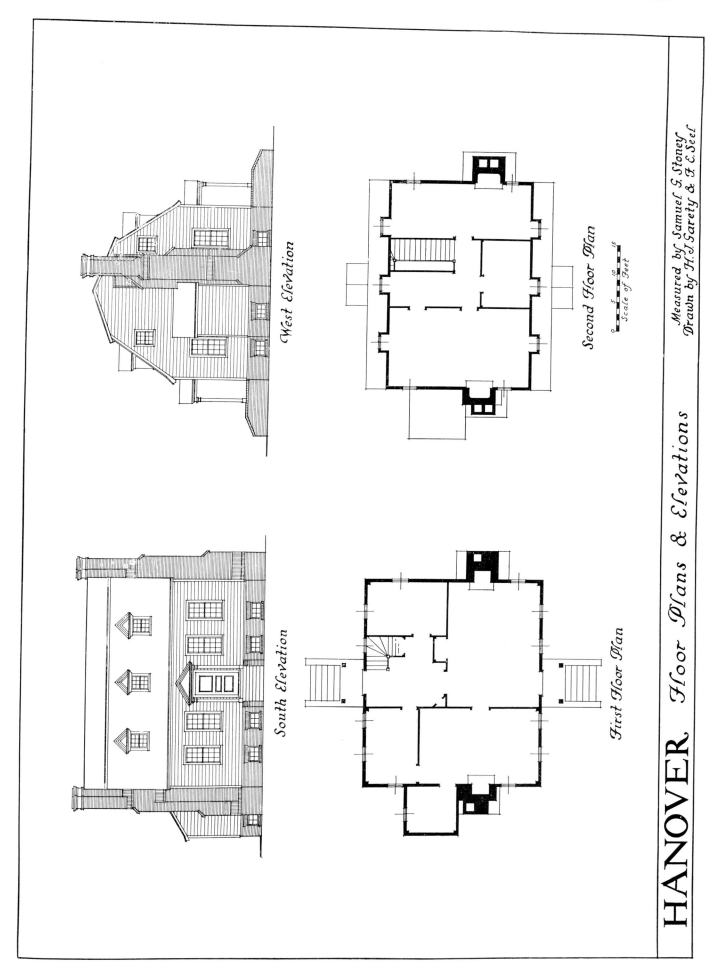

West Elevation

Second Floor Plan

0 5 10 15
Scale of Feet

South Elevation

First Floor Plan

HANOVER Floor Plans & Elevations

Measured by Samuel G. Stoney
Drawn by H. J. Sarety & F. C. Seel

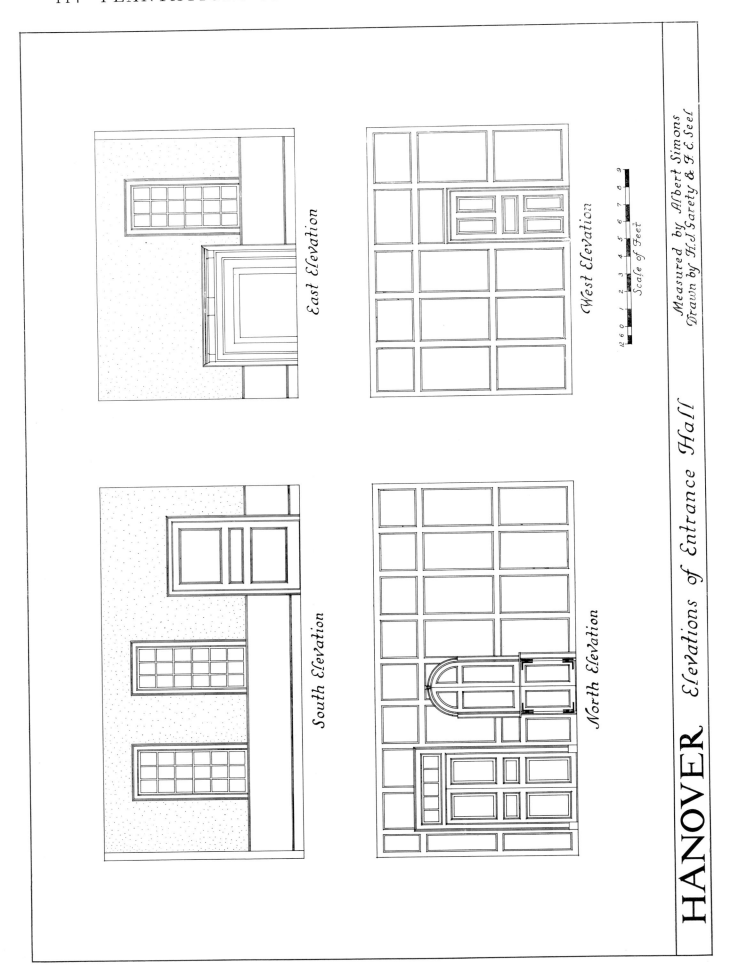

East Elevation

West Elevation

South Elevation

North Elevation

Scale of Feet

Measured by *Albert Simons*
Drawn by *H. J. Sarety & F. E. Seel*

HANOVER *Elevations of Entrance Hall*

CHRIST CHURCH, 1724

C. R. B.

B. J. L.

STRAWBERRY CHAPEL, 1725

BRICK HOUSE, EDISTO, 1725

B. J. L.

B. J. L.

BRICK HOUSE, EDISTO

BRICK HOUSE, EDISTO

B. J. L.

BRICK HOUSE, EDISTO, Bed Room, Second Floor   B. J. L.

BRICK HOUSE, EDISTO, Drawing Room   B. J. L.

EXETER, 1726   F. B. J.

B. J. L.

EXETER

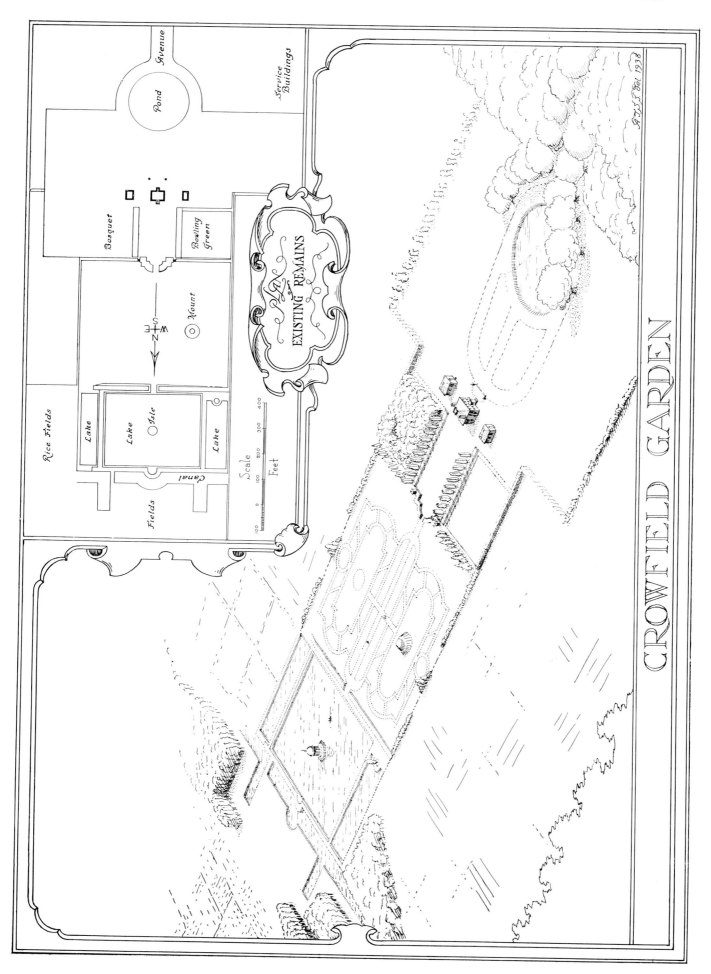

CROWFIELD GARDEN

EXISTING REMAINS

Avenue

Pond

Service Buildings

Bosquet

Bowling Green

Mount

Rice Fields

Lake

Lake

Lake

Isle

Canal

Fields

Scale

0 100 200 300 400

Feet

B. J. L.

FENWICK HALL, 1730, Before Restoration

B. J. L.

FENWICK HALL

FENWICK HALL, North East Room   F. B. J.

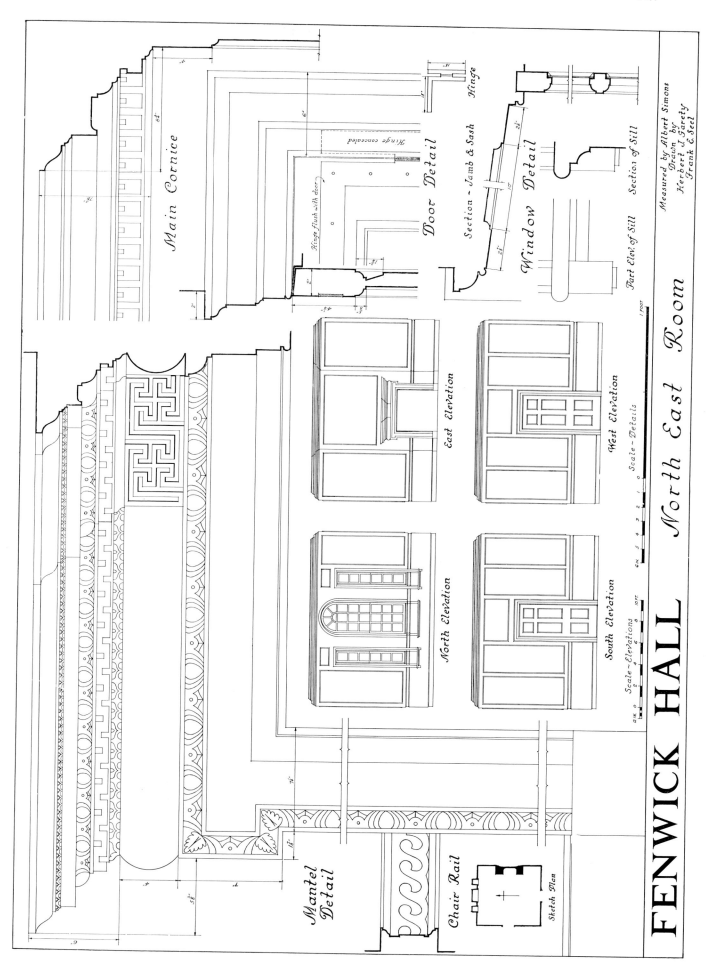

Main Cornice

Door Detail

Section – Jamb & Sash

Hinge

Window Detail

Part Elev. of Sill   Section of Sill

Mantel Detail

Chair Rail

Sketch Plan

East Elevation

West Elevation

North Elevation

South Elevation

Scale – Elevations

Scale – Details

Measured by Albert Simons
Drawn by
Herbert J. Garelty
Frank G. Seel

FENWICK HALL   *North East Room*

FENWICK HALL, South East Room

F. B. J.

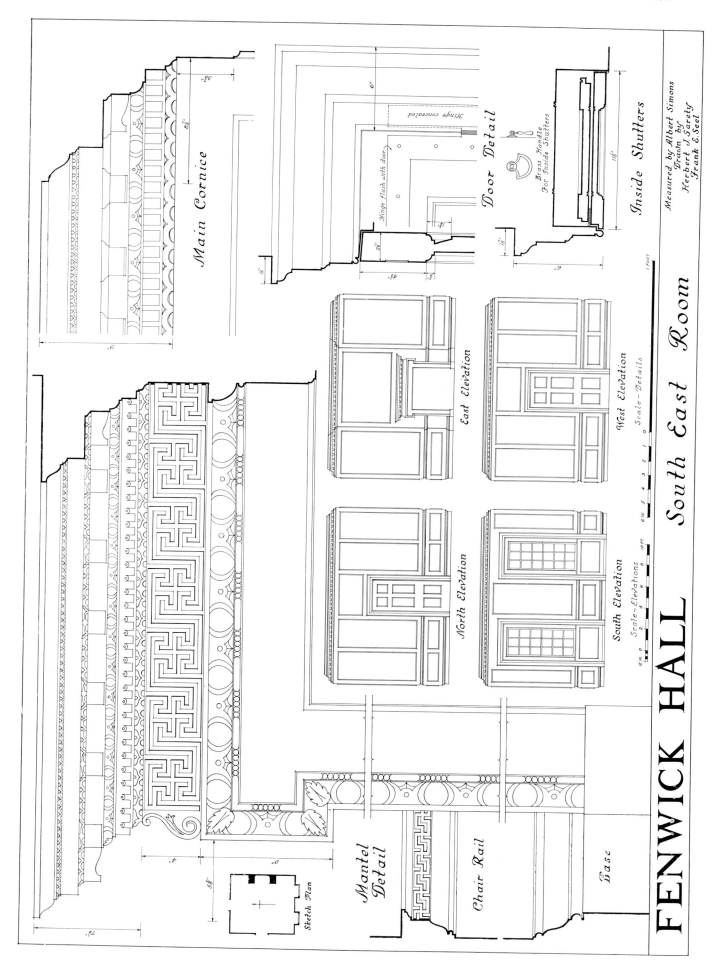

Main Cornice

Door Detail

Inside Shutters

Brass Handle
For Inside Shutters

Hinge concealed

Hinge flush with door

Measured by Albert Simons
Drawn by
Herbert J. Garety
Frank E. Seel

East Elevation

West Elevation

Scale - Details

North Elevation

South Elevation

Scale - Elevations

Mantel
Detail

Chair Rail

Base

Sketch Plan

FENWICK HALL *South East Room*

F. B. J.

FENWICK HALL, Entrance Hall

FENWICK HALL, Entrance Hall

F. B. J.

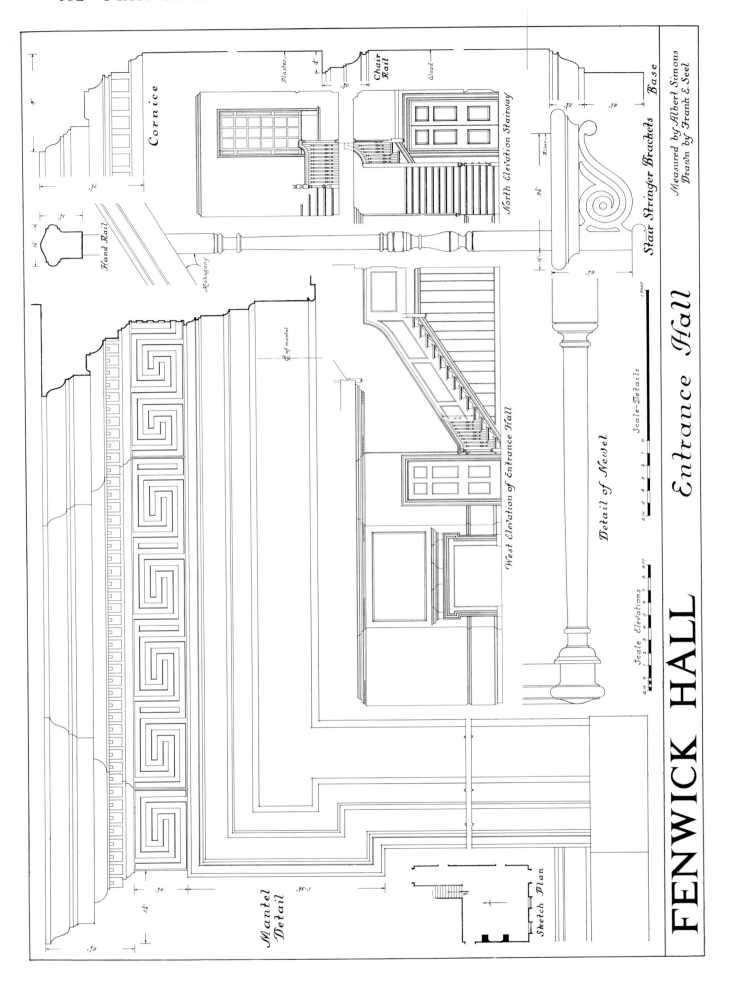

FENWICK HALL Entrance Hall

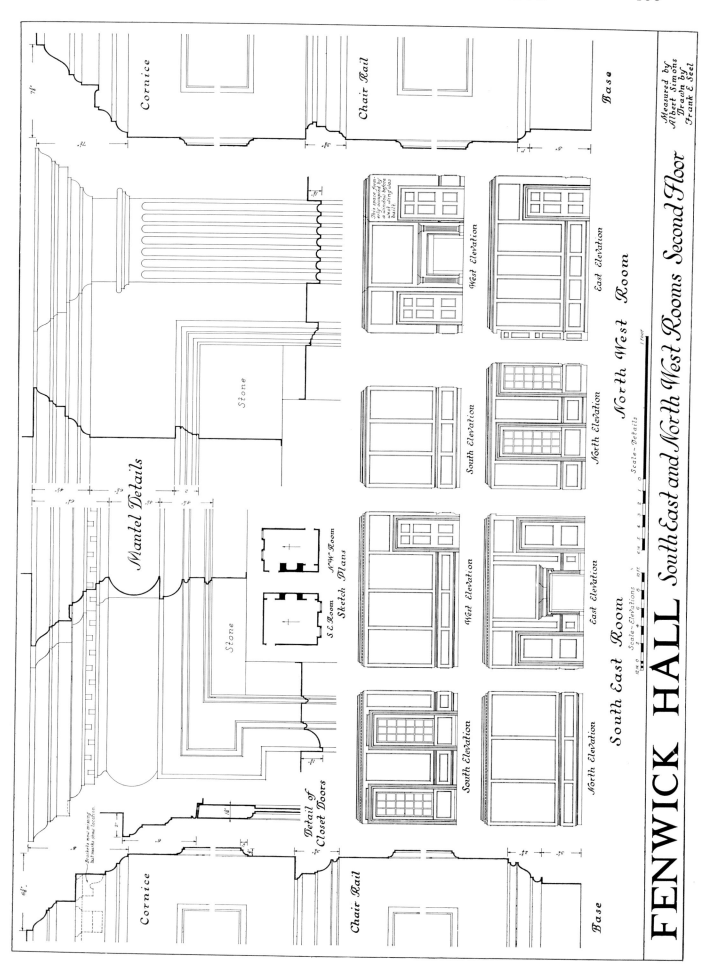

FENWICK HALL *South East and North West Rooms Second Floor*

Measured by Albert Simons
Drawn by Frank E. Seel

F. B. J.

FENWICK HALL, South West Room, Octagonal Wing

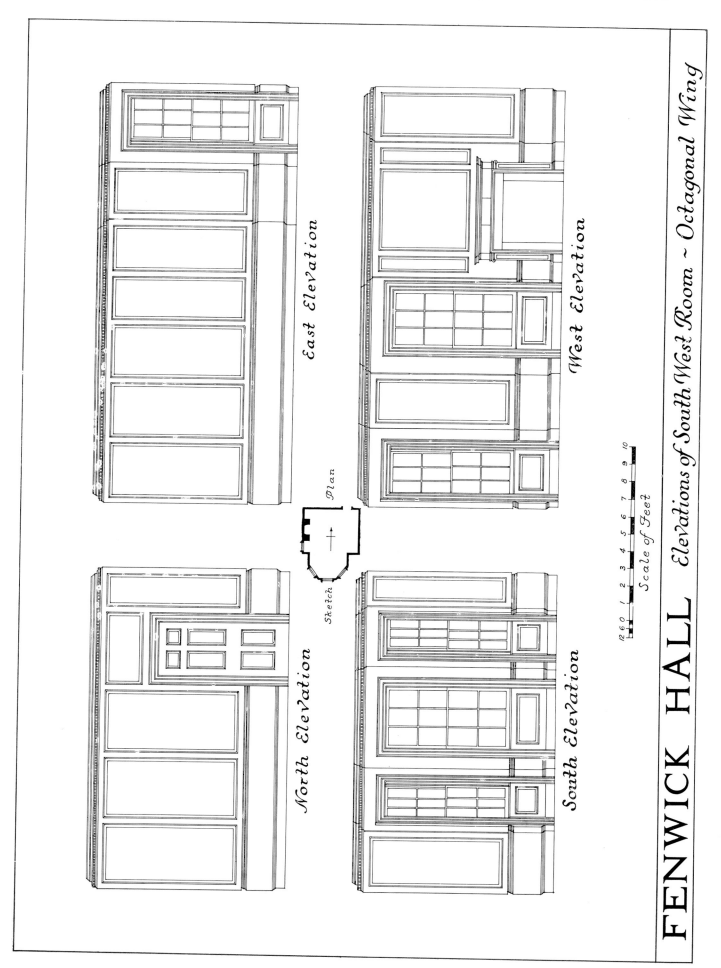

East Elevation

West Elevation

North Elevation

South Elevation

Plan

Sketch

Scale of Feet

FENWICK HALL Elevations of South West Room ~ Octagonal Wing

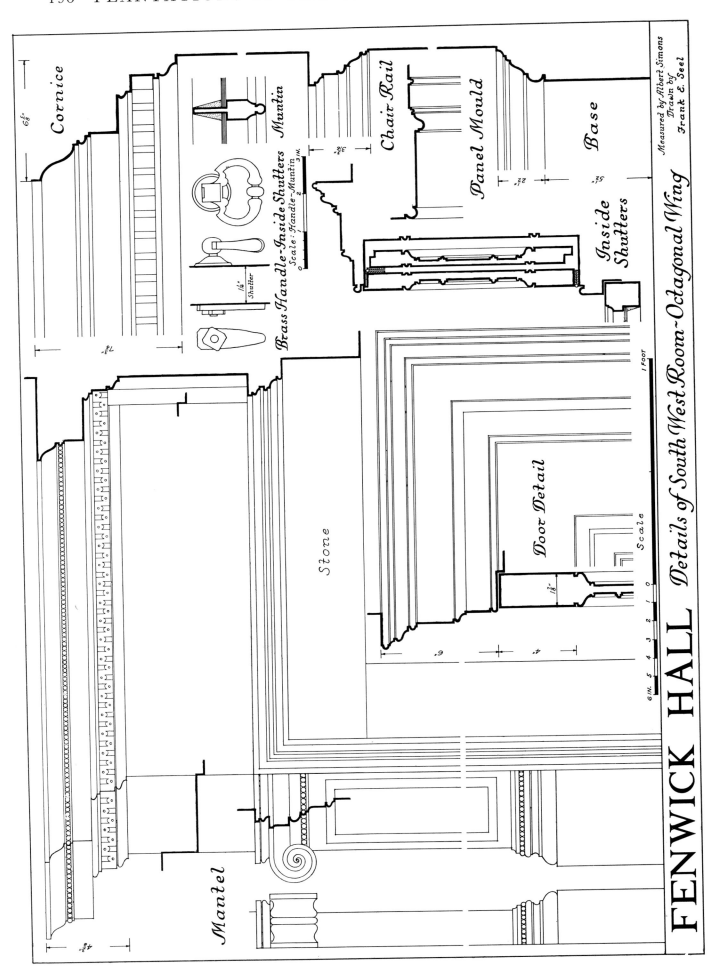

Cornice

Muntin

Chair Rail

Panel Mould

Base

Brass Handle~Inside Shutters

Scale: Handle~Muntin

Inside Shutters

Stone

Door Detail

Scale

Mantel

FENWICK HALL Details of South West Room~Octagonal Wing

Measured by Albert Simons
Drawn by
Frank E. Seel

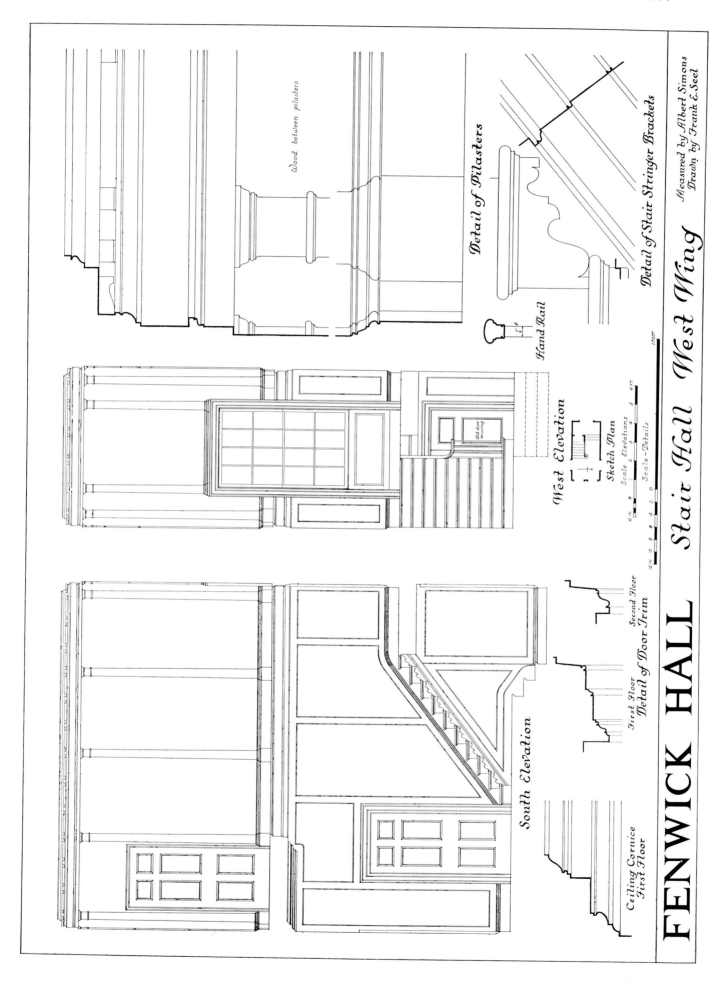

Wood between pilasters

Detail of Pilasters

Hand Rail

Detail of Stair Stringer Brackets

West Elevation

Old door missing

Sketch Plan

Scale Elevations

Scale~Details

Measured by Albert Simons
Drawn by Frank E. Seel

Stair Hall West Wing

Second Floor

First Floor
Detail of Door Trim

South Elevation

Ceiling Cornice
First Floor

FENWICK HALL

FAIRFIELD, 1730, Land Side   F. B. J.

FAIRFIELD, River Side   B. J. L.

HAMPTON, 1735

F. B. J.

F. B. J.

HAMPTON

B. J. L.

HAMPTON

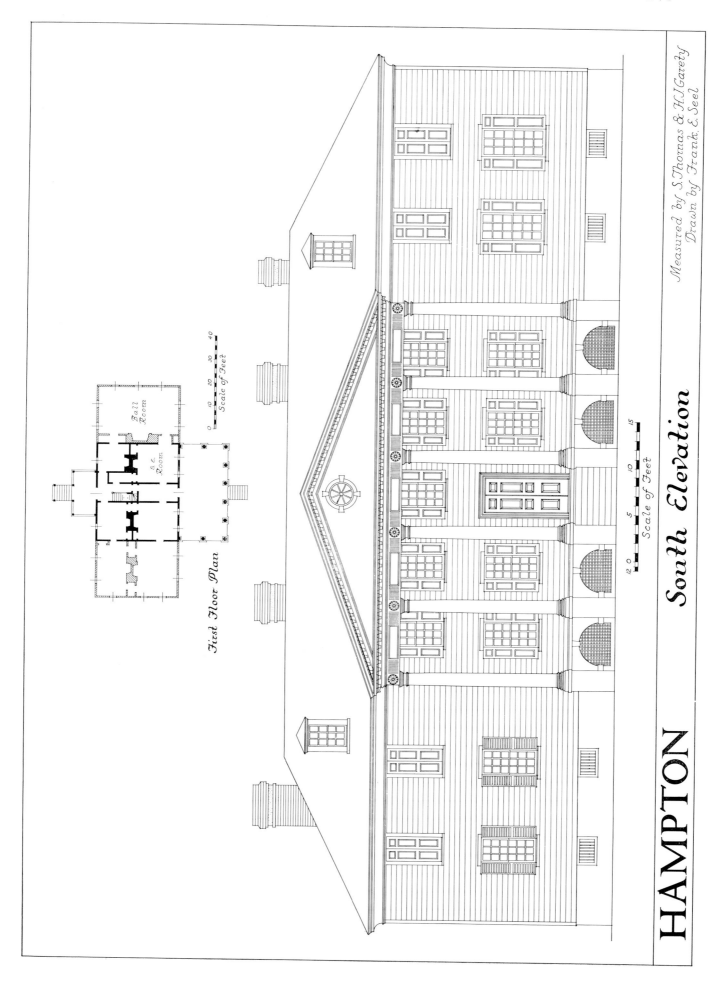

First Floor Plan

Scale of Feet
0 10 20 30 40

Measured by S. Thomas & H.J. Garetly
Drawn by Frank E. Seel

Scale of Feet
12 0 5 10 15

HAMPTON South Elevation

HAMPTON, Ball Room

B. J. L.

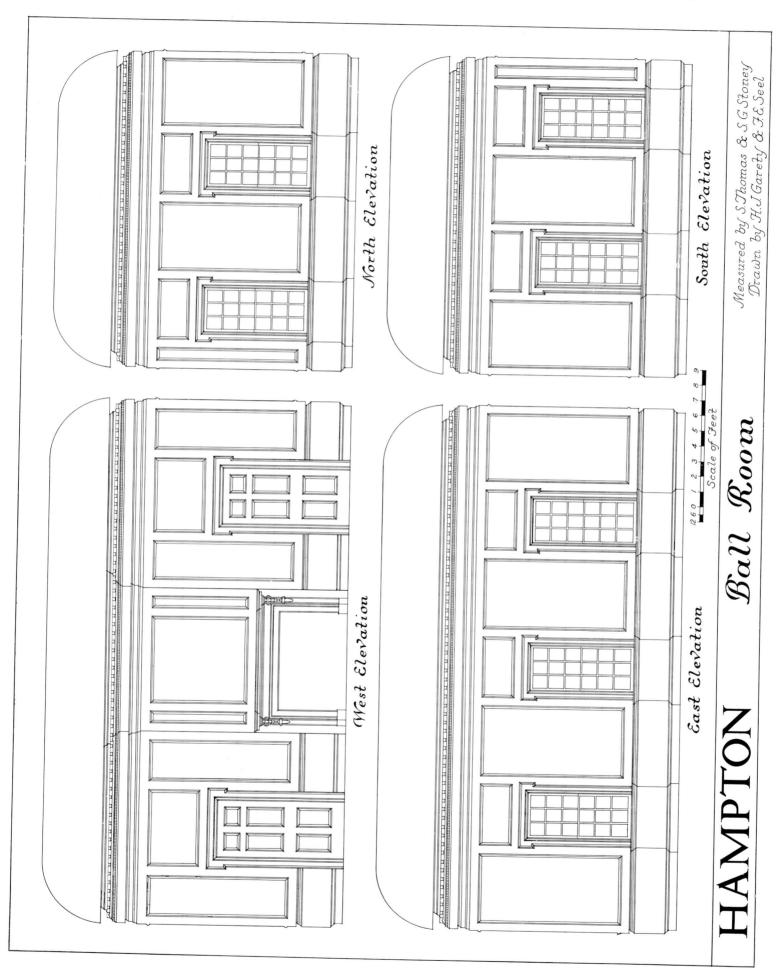

North Elevation

South Elevation

West Elevation

East Elevation

Scale of Feet

Measured by S.Thomas & S.G.Stoney
Drawn by H.J.Garety & F.E.Seel

HAMPTON   Ball Room

F. B. J.

HAMPTON, South East Room

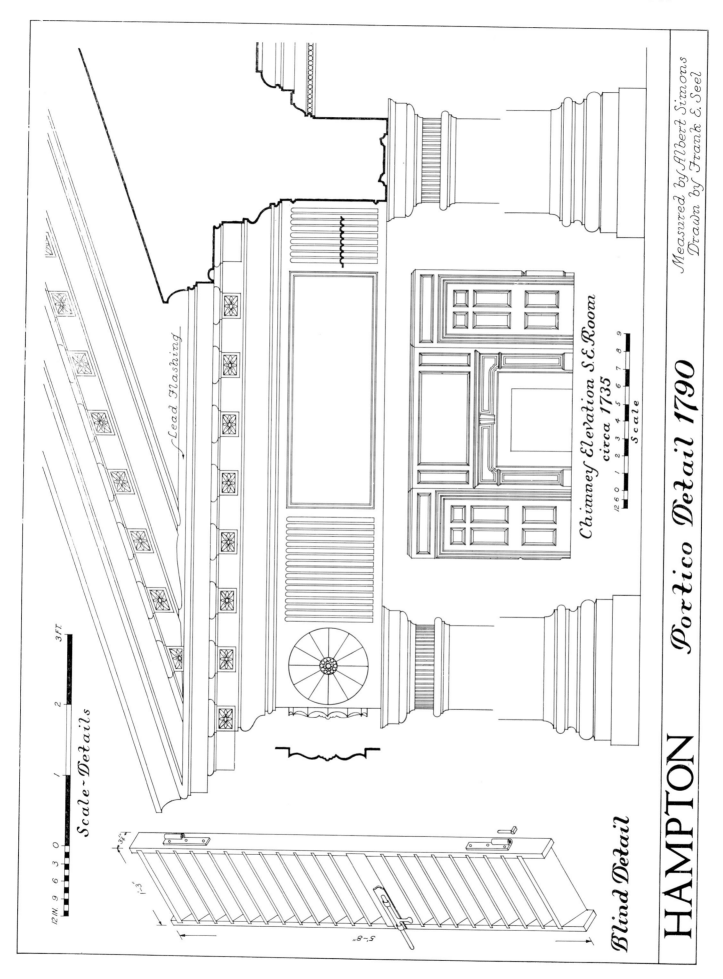

Lead Flashing

Scale~Details

12 IN 9 6 3 0 1 2 3 FT

Chimney Elevation S.E.Room
circa 1735

12 6 0 1 2 3 4 5 6 7 8 9
Scale

Measured by Albert Simons
Drawn by Frank E. Seel

Blind Detail

HAMPTON Portico Detail 1790

DRAYTON HALL, 1738, Land Side

B. J. L.

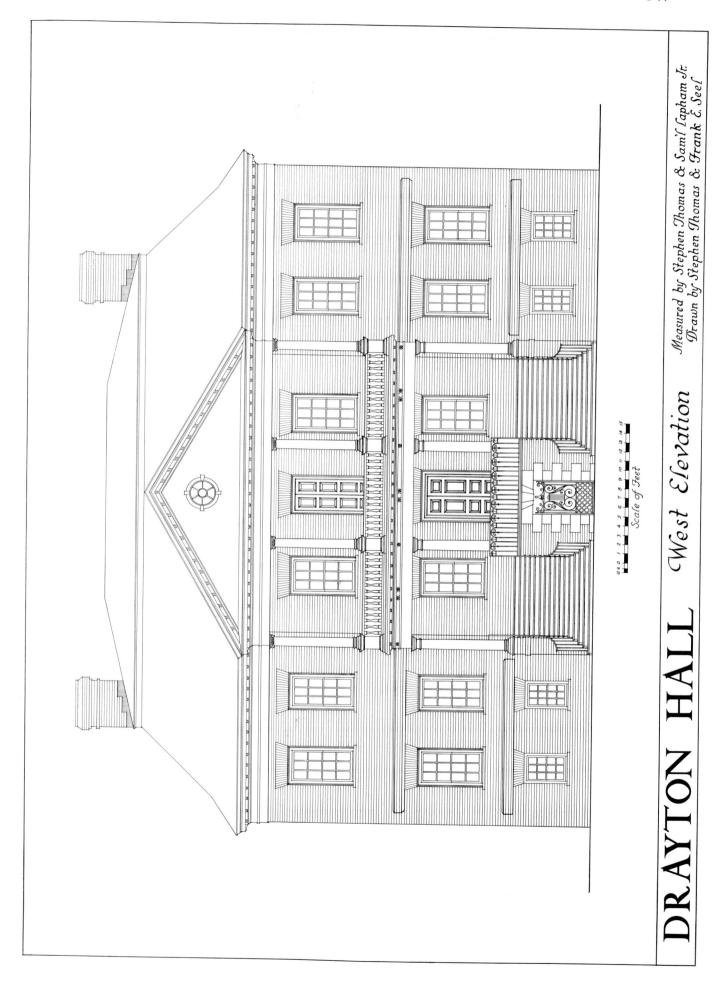

DRAYTON HALL   *West Elevation*

Scale of Feet

Measured by Stephen Thomas & Sam'l Lapham Jr.
Drawn by Stephen Thomas & Frank E. Seel

DRAYTON HALL, River Side

F. B. J.

DRAYTON HALL East Elevation

Measured by Stephen Thomas & Saml Lapham Jr.
Drawn by Stephen Thomas & Frank E. Seel

Scale of Feet

DRAYTON HALL   F. B. J.

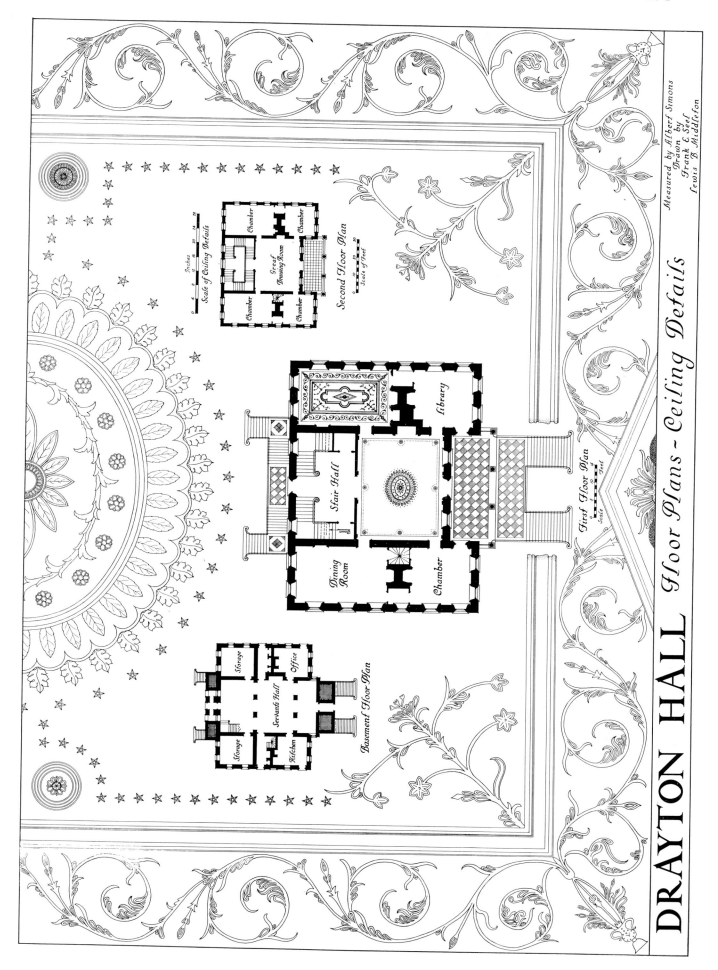

DRAYTON HALL *Floor Plans ~ Ceiling Details*

Measured by Albert Simons
Drawn by Frank E. Seel
Lewis B. Middleton

Second Floor Plan

Chamber

Chamber

Great Drawing Room

Chamber

Chamber

Scale of Ceiling Details

Inches

Scale of Feet

Library

Stair Hall

Dining Room

Chamber

First Floor Plan

Scale Feet

Storage

Office

Servants Hall

Storage

Kitchen

Basement Floor Plan

F. B. J.

DRAYTON HALL, Entrance Hall

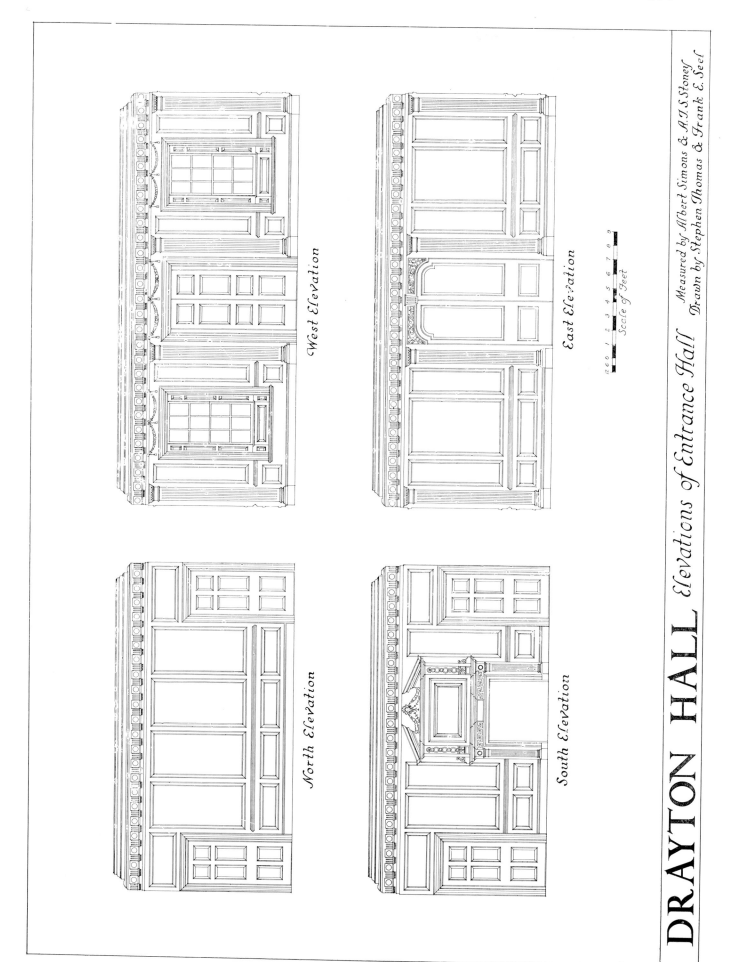

West Elevation

East Elevation

North Elevation

South Elevation

R&O 1 2 3 4 5 6 7 8 9
Scale of Feet

DRAYTON HALL *Elevations of Entrance Hall*

Measured by Albert Simons & A.T.S Stoney
Drawn by Stephen Thomas & Frank E. Seel

DRAYTON HALL, Entrance Hall   F. B. J.

DRAYTON HALL, Entrance Hall   F. B. J.

F. B. J.

DRAYTON HALL, Small Drawing Room

South Elevation

Details

West Elevation

Scale of Feet

Scale of Inches

Measured by H. J. Garety
Drawn by
Frank E. Seel

DRAYTON HALL Staircase

F. B. J.

DRAYTON HALL, Small Drawing Room

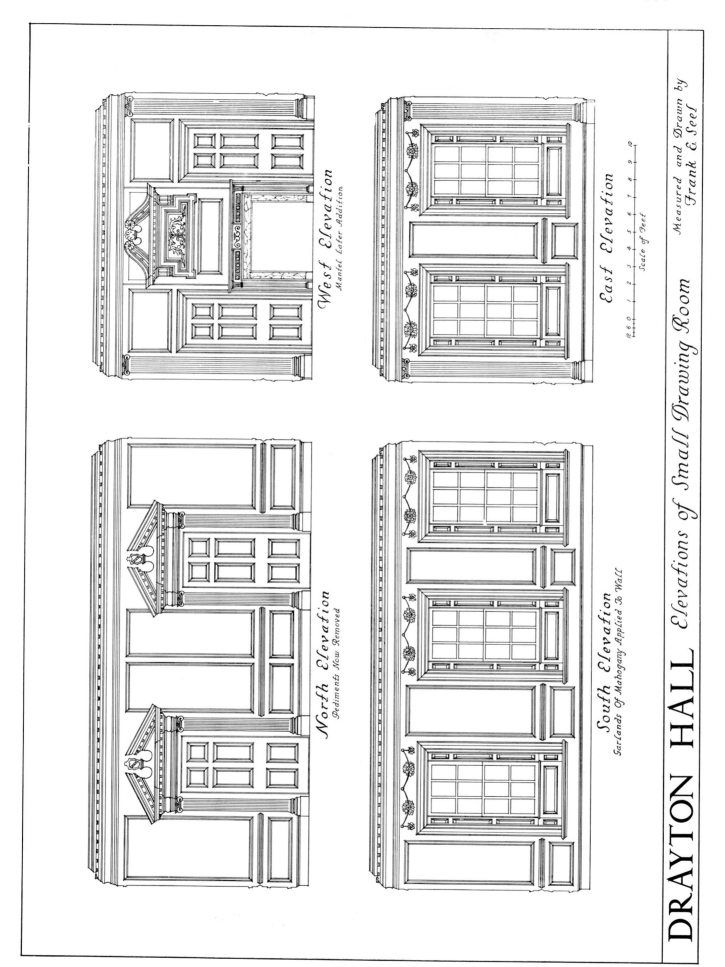

West Elevation
Mantel Later Addition

East Elevation

Scale of Feet
12 6 0 1 2 3 4 5 6 7 8 9 10

Measured and Drawn by
Frank E. Seel

North Elevation
Pediments Now Removed

South Elevation
Garlands Of Mahogany Applied To Wall

DRAYTON HALL *Elevations of Small Drawing Room*

F. B. J.

DRAYTON HALL, Drawing Room, Second Floor

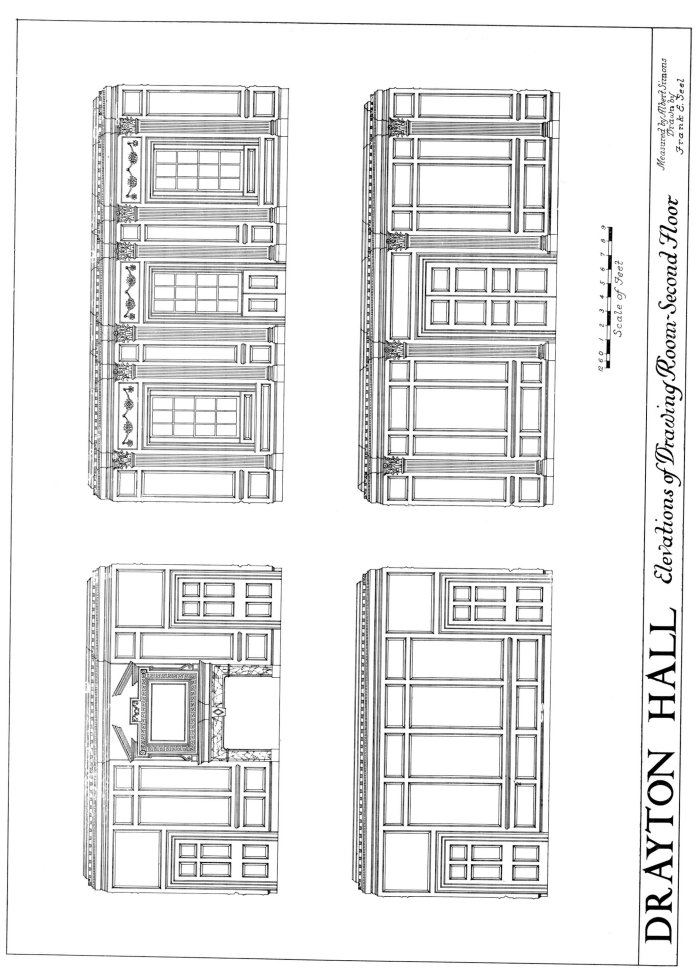

Scale of Feet

DRAYTON HALL *Elevations of Drawing Room~Second Floor*

Measured by Albert Simons
Drawn by
Frank E. Feel

DRAYTON HALL, Drawing Room, Second Floor

F. B. J.

DRAYTON HALL, Dining Room   F. B. J.

B. J. L.

OAKLAND, 1740, Dining Room

B. J. L.

COMINGTEE, 1738

C. R. B.

OAKLAND

B. J. L.

OAKLAND, Kitchen

B. J. L.

TOM SEABROOK'S HOUSE, 1740

F. B. J.

PRINCE WILLIAM'S CHURCH, SHELDON, 1753, West Side

F. B. J.

PRINCE WILLIAM'S CHURCH, SHELDON, South Side

PRINCE WILLIAM'S CHURCH, SHELDON

F. B. J.

East Elevation

South Elevation

West Elevation

Scale of Elevations

Arms of
John Bull Esq.

End Elevation

End Elevation

Side Elevation

Tomb of John and Mary Ball

Side Elevation

Tomb of Mary Middleton

Scale of Tombs

Scale of Details

Ruins and Tombs

Measured by Robert N. S. and Pall. F. Whitelaw,
Samuel G. Stoney and Albert Simons.
Drawn by Frank E. Seel

PRINCE WILLIAM'S PARISH CHURCH ~ SHELDON

F. B. J.

MIDDLETON PLACE, 1755, The River and the Rice Mill

B. J. L.

MIDDLETON PLACE, Mill Pond and the Spring House

MIDDLETON PLACE, The Tomb   F. B. J.

Charleston Road

N

Legend
A. The Mount
B. The Great Oak
C. The Main Dwelling
D. The Tomb
E. The Kitchen
F. The Spring House
G. The Rice Mill

Scale of Feet
0   100   200

Plan Showing
Site of Garden
on River

Charleston Road

Ashley River

Stable

Servants'
Quarters

Rice Fields

River

MIDDLETON
PLACE
IN SOUTH CAROLINA

H.T.S.Stoney
surv. & del.
1938.

B. J. L.

MIDDLETON PLACE, South Flanker, West Side

MIDDLETON PLACE, South Flanker, East Side

B. J. L.

MIDDLETON PLACE, The Great Oak

F. B. J.

NORTH CHACHAN, 1760, Stable   F. B. J.

BIGGIN CHURCH, 1761   B. J. L.

POMPION HILL CHAPEL, 1763

F. B. J.

POMPION HILL CHAPEL

F. B. J.

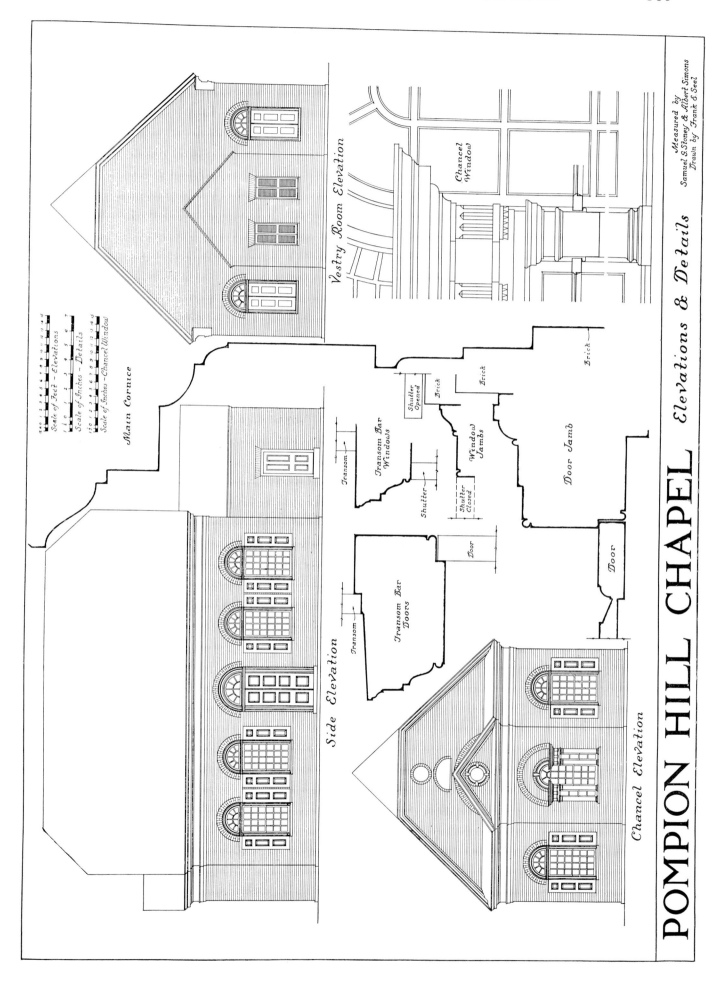

Vestry Room Elevation

Chancel Window

Main Cornice

Scale of Feet ~ Elevations

Scale of Inches ~ Details

Scale of Inches ~ Chancel Window

Transom

Transom Bar
Windows

Shutter

Shutter
Closed

Window
Jambs

Shutter
Opened

Brick

Brick

Brick

Brick

Door Jamb

Door

Door

Transom

Transom Bar
Doors

Side Elevation

Chancel Elevation

POMPION HILL CHAPEL *Elevations & Details*

Measured by
Samuel S. Stoney & Albert Simons
Drawn by Frank E. Seel

POMPION HILL CHAPEL   F. B. J.

POMPION HILL CHAPEL   F. B. J.

B. J. L.

ST. STEPHEN'S CHURCH, 1767

ST. STEPHEN'S CHURCH Elevation of Chancel

Measured by
Albert Simons & Frank E. Seel
Drawn by Frank E. Seel

ST. JAMES' CHURCH, SANTEE, 1768

B. J. L.

ST. JAMES' CHURCH, SANTEE

B. J. L.

LEWISFIELD, 1774   B. J. L.

OTRANTO, 1790   B. J. L.

THE BLUFF, 1790   B. J. L.

HARRIETTA, 1797, Entrance Side   F. B. J.

HARRIETTA, Garden Side   F. B. J.

HARRIETTA

F. B. J.

HARRIETTA, Doors on Garden Side   F. B. J.

HARRIETTA, Drawing Room

F. B. J.

HARRIETTA, Dining Room

F. B. J.

HARRIETTA, Dining Room   F. B. J.

HARRIETTA, Rice Field   F. B. J.

BELVIDERE, 1800, River Side

B. J. L.

BELVIDERE, Land Side   B. J. L.

BELVIDERE   B. J. L.

B. J. L.

BELVIDERE, Ball Room

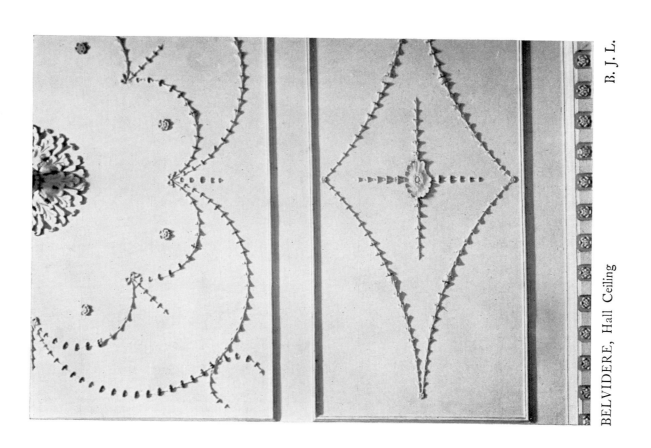

B. J. L.

BELVIDERE, Hall Ceiling

LOWNDES' GROVE, 1803   F. B. J.

THE ROCKS, 1805, Rear Elevation

F. B. J.

THE ROCKS, Drawing Room   F. B. J.

WAPPAOOLA, 1806   B. J. L.

WAPPAOOLA   B. J. L.

WAPPAOOLA   B. J. L.

EUTAW, 1808

B. J. L.

F. B. J.

EUTAW, The Lodge

EUTAW, Rear Elevation   B. J. L.

EUTAW, The Lodge   F. B. J.

EUTAW, Parlor   F. B. J.

MARSHLANDS, 1810, South Side

B. J. L.

B. J. L.

MARSHLANDS

B. J. L.

MARSHLANDS, North Side

F. B. J.

MARSHLANDS, Drawing Room

MARSHLANDS   B. J. L.

MARSHLANDS   B. J. L.

B. J. L.

WILLIAM SEABROOK'S HOUSE, 1810

WILLIAM SEABROOK'S HOUSE   B. J. L.

WILLIAM SEABROOK'S HOUSE   B. J. L.

THE ELMS, 1810, Garden Side

B. J. L.

SPRINGFIELD, 1818   B. J. L.

SPRINGFIELD, Drawing Room

B. J. L.

F. B. J.

TOMOTLEY AVENUE, 1820

OPHIR, 1810   B. J. L.

WHITE HALL, 1822   B. J. L.

B. J. L.

WHITE HALL

B. J. L.

WHITE HALL, The Old Entrance

LAWSON'S POND, 1823

B. J. L.

THE WEDGE, 1826, North Side Before Restoration

B. J. L.

THE WEDGE, South Side

F. B. J.

DEAN HALL, 1827   B. J. L.

DEAN HALL   B. J. L.

THE GROVE, 1828, Before Restoration B. J. L.

SOMERSET, 1852 B. J. L.

THE LAUNCH, 1830, Land Side   B. J. L.

THE LAUNCH, Water Side   B. J. L.

PRESBYTERIAN CHURCH, EDISTO, 1831

B. J. L.

PRESBYTERIAN CHURCH, EDISTO   B. J. L.

SOMERTON, 1836

B. J. L.

B. J. L.

SOMERTON

MAGNOLIA GARDENS, 1840

F. B. J.

B. J. L.

BOONE HALL, 1843, Negro Street

F. B. J.

BOONE HALL, Negro Street

B. J. L.

GIPPY, 1852, After Restoration

PROSPECT HILL, PON PON, 1878   B. J. L.

PROSPECT HILL, PON PON   B. J. L.

CHRONOLOGICAL INDEX

1686—Medway, 47
1699—Middleburg, 48
1706—St. Andrew's Church, 49
1708—St. James' Church, Goose Creek, 50
1714—Mulberry, 51
1720—Hanover, 52
1724—Christ Church, 53
1725—Strawberry Chapel, 54
1725—Brick House, Edisto, 54
1726—Exeter, 55
1730—Crowfield, 56
1730—Fenwick Hall, 57
1730 (c.)—Fairfield, 59
1735—Hampton, 59
1738—Drayton Hall, 61
1738—Comingtee, 62
1740—Oakland, 62
1740—Tom Seabrook's House, 62
1753—Prince William's Church, Sheldon, 63
1755—Middleton Place, 64
1760—North Chachan, 65
1761—Biggin Church, 66
1763—Pompion Hill Chapel, 67
1767—St. Stephen's Church, 68
1768—St. James' Church, 69
1774—Lewisfield, 69
1790—Otranto, 71
1790—The Bluff, 71

1797—Harrietta, 71
1797—El Dorado, 73
1800—Belvidere, 74
1803—Lowndes' Grove, 74
1805—The Rocks, 75
1806—Wappaoola, 75
1807—Mount Hope, 76
1808—Eutaw, 76
1810—Marshlands, 77
1810—Ophir, 77
1810—William Seabrook's House, 78
1810—The Elms, 79
1818—Springfield, 80
1820—Tomotley, 80
1822—White Hall, 81
1823—Lawson's Pond, 81
1826—The Wedge, 81
1827—Dean Hall, 82
1828—The Grove, 83
1830—The Launch, 83
1831—Presbyterian Church, Edisto, 84
1836—Somerton, 84
1840—Magnolia Gardens, 85
1843—Boone Hall, 85
1852—Gippy, 86
1852—Somerset, 87
1878—Prospect Hill, 87

GENERAL INDEX

Abney family, 72
Absenteeism, 35, 36, 41
Acknowledgment, 5
Adam Brothers, architecture, 45; influence, 46; mantels, 61; Marshlands style 74, 77
Adam, Robert, 60
Aiken, Governor William, 41
Albany, 20
Albemarle, Duke of, 13, 22
American Council of Learned Societies, 5, 9
Anglican Church, first, 66
Antigua, 28, 45, 51; plantation tongue, 16
Antilles, 15, 16, 49
Antipaedobaptists, 18, 87
Archdale Hall, 45
Architects, Brendon, 51; Curtis, 84; Hoban, 78; Howells, 1, 7; Simons and Lapham, 1, 7; of St. Stephen's unidentified, 68
Architecture, Adam, 45, 60, 74, 77; age identification, 47; Charleston houses (double, single), 48; Charleston influence, 40, 45; Doric, 55, 82, 84; Dutch, 47, 53; early building, 23; effect of Revolution, 37; European, 49, 70; French, 55; gouge work, 45, 77, 80; Greek Revival, 46, 66, 82, 83; Low Country Augustan Age, 24; periods, 27; polygonal rooms, 45, 76, 83; rice prosperity, 34; St. John's, 75, 77, 80, 81; tabby, 45, 73; trends, 44-46; war toll (see also Devastation), 30; West Indian, 48, 55, 70
Argyll, Duke of, son's marriage, 29
Ashby, John, 67
Ashley-Cooper, Anthony, 13; colonization, 14, 15, 17; Constitution (with Locke), 13, 14; Indian policy, 21; legislation, 26; plantation, 14, 52
Ashley River, Federal invasion, 61; name, 15; plantations, 45, 57, 61, 64, 74, 85; St. Andrew's Parish, 49; St. Giles Barony, 14
Augustan Age in Low Country, 24
avenues, Boone Hall, 86; Crowfield, 56, 57; Medway, 48; Tomotley, 80
Axson, William, 67, 68
Azalea indica, 85

Back River, 47, 67, 82
Bahamas, 15, 38
Baker house, 45
Ball, Elias, 62
Ball, John, 77
Ball, Keating Simons, 54
Ball, Marie Guerin, 49
Balston Spa, 36
Banks, Charles Richard, 89
Baptists, 18, 26, 87; Edisto, 26
Barbadians, 12, 19; Draytons, 61; Goose Creek, 19, 50; Middletons, 56, 71; See West Indians
Barbadoes, 12, 15, 45, 49; plantation dialect, 16; piazzas, 46
Barnum, William Henry, 76
Barnwell, Edward, 87
baronies, Fairlawn, 69, 86; Quinby, 67; St. Giles, 14; Wadboo, 31
baroque style, 50, 51, 65

Beaufort, 17, 45, 73
Bellinger, Edmund, baronial grant, 81
Belvidere, 74; illustrations, 199-201; St. John's Berkeley, 45, 76
Benison, Captain George, 62
Bennett, John, author, 48
Berkeley Country Club, 56
Berkeley County, see St. John's
Berkeley, Lord, 13
Berkeley, Sir William, 13
Bermuda, 15
BIGGIN CHURCH, 66, 67; illustrations, 180; plan, 66; war use, 31, 66
Blanchard, Mr. and Mrs. Claude W., 59
Blue Ridge, resorts, 36
BLUFF, THE, 71; illustration, 191
BOONE HALL, 85, 86; illustrations 234, 235
Boone, Major John, land grant, 85
Boone, Joseph, 85
Boston Museum of Fine Arts, 79
Bostwick, Mr. G. H., 81
Bourbons, conquest of Spain, 20
Brawley, Mrs. Marion, 52
Brendon, Charles, 51
brick, Boston, 54; "Carolina Grey", 48; early industry, 23; English bond, 52, 57; Flemish bond, 57; Horlbeck yard, 86; Medway, 48, 82; Parnassus Plantation, 48; sun-dried, 75; Van Arrsens', 23, 48
BRICK HOUSE, 44, 46, 54, 55, 59; illustrations, 117-120; plan, 55; porch, 46
Bridgetown, Barbadoes, 46
Briggs, Loutrel W., 52
Broughton, Thomas, 27, 51, 52; English family estate, 56
building, indigo age, 28; rice prosperity, 34; See Architecture
Bull, John, family, 63
Bull, Lt. Governors, 63
Bull, Stephen, 63
Butler, Hugh, 55

Cacique, 14, 19, 47, 67
Cain family, 87
Cain, William, 87
Calvinists, 18; Up-Country, 32
Camellia japonica, 49,
Canoes, 16, 17
Cape Fear, 19
Cape Fear River, 13
Cape Hatteras, 19
Cape Lookout, 19
Caribbean, pirates, 22
Carolina, 13, 16; expansion, 20; titles, 14, 19
Carolina, ship, 62, 63
Carolina Art Association, 1, 2, 5, 9
Carpenter-builders, importation, 44
Carson, James Petigru, 82
Carson, William Augustus, 82
Carteret, Sir George, 13
Catholics, Irish, 18
Chachan, see NORTH CHACHAN
Chadwick, Mr. and Mrs. Elbridge Gerry, 82

Champlin, George, 80, 81

chapels of ease, St. Thomas & St. Denis, 67; Strawberry, 54

Chapman, Mr. and Mrs. Clarence E., 51, 52

Charles II, 13,

Charles IX of France, 13

Charlesfort, Huguenot settlement, 11

Charleston, Confederate War siege, 41; evacuation, 41; freedom of worship, 26; harbor, 15, 16, 17, 41; house styles, 73, 76; influence on architecture, 44; loss of government seat, 31; metropolis, 35; name, 31; planning, 14, 15; piazzas, 46; reverence for Greek form, 82

Charleston Country Club, 74

Charleston Free Library, 40

Charleston Library Society, 5

Charleston Museum, 73

Charles-Town, defenses, 20; early building, 23; early character, 18; early Revolutionary victory, 29; early trade, 16; fires, 24; Indian trade, 20; metropolis, 17; name change, 31; Revolutionary siege, 30; settlement, 15; West Indian migration, 16

Cheves, Langdon, 5

Child, James, 54

Childsbury, proposed town, 54

Chisolm, Susan, 83

Chisolm, Dr. Robert Trail, 83

CHRIST CHURCH, 53; illustration, 115; parish, 62; vestry, 53

Church of England, see Establishment

churches, St. Andrew's, 49; Biggin Church, 66, 67; building boom, 28; burned, 53, 63, 66; Christ Church, 53; St. James', Goose Creek, 50, 51; St. James', Santee, 68, 69; plantation customs, 63, 67, 68, 84; Pompion Hill, 45, 67; Presbyterian, 84; Prince William's, 63; profanation by British, 31; Strawberry, 54; war destruction, 30, 53, 63, 66

Clarendon, Earl of, 13

Clemson College, School of Architecture, 43, 53

Clinton, Sir Henry, map, 74

College of Charleston, 77, 84

Colleton, Anne, 55

Colleton family, use of marl, 23; war toll of estates, 31

Colleton, Sir John, 12, 13, 16, 66

Colleton, Sir Peter, 52

colonization, 11, 14, 15

Columbia, capital, 31, 40, 41

columns, The Elms, 80; The Grove, 83; Presbyterian Church, 84; Somerton, 85; (and posts) evolution, 46

Combahee River, 73; rice prosperity, 39

Combe-in-Tene, 62

Coming, Affra Harleston, 62

Coming, John, 62

COMINGTEE, 54, 62; illustration, 166

Commissary, Church, 26

Commissioners of Public Works, 80

Confederate War, 41, 78; See Devastation

Connor, J. Rutledge, 43, 75

Constitution, Locke's Fundamental, 13, 14, 19

Convention, Declaration of Independence, 30

Cooper River, British retreat, 66; places: Belvidere, 74, Childsbury, 54, Comingtee, 62, Dean Hall, 82, Gippy, 86, Hanover, 52, Lewisfield, 69, Marshlands, 77, Medway, 47, Mulberry, 51, North Chachan, 55, Pompion Hill Chapel, 67, Strawberry Chapel, 54, The Bluff, 71; T, 62, 82; swamps, 52

Copley, Izard portrait, 79

Cordes, Antoine, 65

Cordes, Francis, 65, 66

Cordes, James, 65

Cordes, Samuel, 39

cotton, black seed, 37, 39; decline, 42; first planting, 15; gin, 36; green seed, 38; history, 27; influence, 39; prosperity, 32, 38, 40; Sea-Island strains, 37, 40

Couturier, Elias F., 81

Covenanters, Scotch, 18

Craven, Earl of, 13

CROWFIELD, 24, 29, 44, 56, 57, 64, 73; illustrations, 123; plan, 57

Cumberland, Duke of, 63

Curtis, E. M., 84

Cypress Gardens, 82

Dawtaw Island, 45, 73

DEAN HALL, 82; illustration, 226; piazza, 46

de Avilés, Menendez, 11

Declaration of Independence, 30

dedication, 3

DeLancey, Alice, 79

Deloraine, Countess, 25

Dennis, Dr. Edward J., 66

Dennis, Hon. Rembert C., 70

de St. Julien, Paul, 52, 53

"Designs of Inigo Jones", 51

devastation, dilapidation, 26, 42, 79; earthquake, 26, 45, 47, 79; fire, 24, 27, 42, 49, 63, 64, 79, 84, 86, 87; hurricanes, 42; war, 26, 30, (Confederate) 41, 42, 61, 78 (Revolutionary), 63, 66, 73 (Yemassee), 24

Deveaux, Andrew, 28

devices and inscriptions, St. Andrew's, 49; Arms of England, 30, 50; Fairfield, 59; Hanover, 52; Mulberry, 27, 52; Pompion Hill, 67; St. James', Goose Creek, 50; St. Stephen's, 68; Wm. Seabrook's House, 79; South Carolina flag, 30

de Vignon, Sabina, 47

Devonshire, 62

dialect, see Gullah

Dingle, Edward von S., 49

Dissenters, 17, 18, 25, 31

Doar, David, 72

Doar, Stephen, 72

Dodge, Donald D., 79

Dorchester, 18

Dorsetshire, 13

double house, 44

Dover Plantation, 43

Downs, England, 15

Drayton family, 61, 85

DRAYTON HALL, 24, 27, 40, 44, 61; columns, 46; illustrations, 146-165; plan, 151

Drayton, John, 61

Drayton, Rev. John Grimké, 85

Drayton, Thomas, 85

Drayton, William Henry, 61

DuBose, Mrs. Theodore Marion, 48

Dupont, Gideon, 32

Dutch colonists, 18

Eastern Branch, Cooper River, 62, 67

Edict of Nantes, 17

Edisto Island, civic character, 37; house plan, 74; plantations, 45, 59, 62, 78; religion, 26

Edisto River, Federal invasion, 41; plantations, 76, 87; Yemassees, 24

EL DORADO, 44, 45, 73; plan, 73

Elliott, Anne Barnett, 76

ELMS, THE, 45, 79, 80; columns, 46; illustration, 217; plan, 79; polygonal rooms, 45, 83

Emerson, Frances and William, 3, 7, 9

England, architectural influence, 45; Carolina homeland, 29; Church of, See Establishment; rice mills, 34; trade, 28

English, colonists, 15

English Santee, 68

Establishment, 20, 51, 53, 66; Edisto, 26; effect of Revolution, 37; effect on society, 25; opposition in Up Country, 32

European architecture, 70

Eustis, Abraham, 81

EUTAW, 44, 76, 77; illustrations, 207-210

Eutaw Springs, 31, 39, 77

EXETER, 44, 55, 56; illustrations, 121-122; plan, 56

FAIRFIELD, 44, 46, 59, 60, 73; illustrations, 138; piazza, 46

Fairlawn Barony, 52, 55, 69, 86; burned in Revolution, 31; divisions, 69, 86

Federals, 41, 42, 54, 61, 78, 87

Fenwick, Edward, 58

Fenwick, Edward II, 58

FENWICK HALL, 24, 25, 57, 58; illustrations, 124-137; legend, 57; plan, 58; polygonal rooms, 45

Fenwick, John, 25, 29, 58

Fenwick, Robert, 57

fires, See Devastation

Fitch, Jonathan, 49

Fitz Simons, Ellen M., 5

Flat Rock, 36

Florida, 11, 21

Fort Caroline, 11

Fort Motte, 73

Fort Sumter, 41, 48

fortified houses, Mulberry, 51

France, settlement of Louisiana 20; Revolution, 38; wars, 27

Fraser, Charles, 50

freedmen, 42

French, see Huguenots

French-English War, 27

French and Indian War, 27

French Quarter, 26

French Santee, 59, 68

frontiers, 20-24

Fundamental Constitution, 13, 14

Gaillard, Catherine, 81

Gaillard family, 23

Gaillard, Joachim, 23

Gaillard, Peter, 37, 75, 78; cotton prosperity, 39

Garden, Dr. Alexander, 71

Garden, Major, 71

gardenia, 71

gardens, formal, Crowfield, 24; Cypress, 82; Elms, 79; Magnolia, 85; Medway, 48; Middleton, 7, 28, 57, 65

Garrick, villa, 60

Gazette, 31, 65

geology, 17

George-Town, 17, 32

Georgia, black-seed cotton, 38; frontier, 24

"Georgian Period, The", 77

Germans, 24

Gibbes family, 73

Gibbes, John, 58, 74; home destroyed, 30

GIPPY, 86; illustration, 236; plan, 86

Goose Creek, 29, 32, 56, 57, 67, 71; church, See St. James'; missionaries, 50; parish, 28; people, 19, 24, 25, 37, 79, 81; plantations, 56, 71, 79; Yemassee destruction, 24

gouge work, 45, 77, 80

government, see Lords Proprietors, Republic, Royal Government

Governors, Aiken, 41; (lieutenant) Bull, 63; (lieutenant) Cain, 87; Hamilton, 54; Johnson, 27, 67; Lucas (of Antigua), 28; Manning, 40; (acting) Middleton, 56; official residence, 74; Richardson, 40; St. Augustine, 11; Smith, 47

Governor's Creek, 83

Greek architecture, 84

Greek Revival, 46, 66, 82, 83, 84

Greene, General Nathanael, 76

Gregorie, Mr. and Mrs. Ferdinand, 62

Grimball, Paul, 55

Grimké, John, 85

GROVE, THE, 30, 76, 83; columns, 46; illustration, 227; plan, 83; polygonal rooms, 45, 76, 83

Guernsey (cattle), 86

gullah, 16

Hamilton, Paul, 54, 55

Hampton (England), 60

HAMPTON, 59, 60; ballroom, 28, 71, 72; illustrations, 139-145; portico, 27, 28, 44, 46

Hampton, Colonel Wade, 40, 70

HANOVER, 43, 44, 52, 53; illustrations, 112-114

Hanover, House of, 52

Hansa, towns, 34

Harleston, Affra, 62

Harleston, Major Isaac Child, 71

Harleston, John, 62

HARRIETTA, 28, 44, 45, 46, 60, 71, 73; columns, 46; false door, 72; illustrations, 191-198; plan, 72; porch, 46, 60

Harrison, Fairfax, 58

Hastie, C. Norwood, 85

Hastie, J. Drayton, 85

hatchment, Izard, 50

Henri IV, 55

Henry, Mr. and Mrs. R. Carter, 83

Hercules, horse trainer, 77

Heyward, Marie H., 5

Heyward, Nathaniel, 40; town house, 41

Hoban, architect, 78

Holland, architecture, 47; colonists, 18, 47

Hoospa Neck, 63

Horlbeck, Daniel, 86

Horlbeck, Edward, 86

Horlbeck, Henry, 85, 86; children, 86

Horlbeck, Henry II, 86

Horlbeck, John, 85

Horlbeck, John II, 86

Horlbeck, Peter, 85

Horry, Charles Lucas Pinckney (formerly Daniel), 72

Horry, Daniel Huger, 28, 59, 72

Horry, Harriott, 71

Horry, Harriott P., 28, 59, 71

Horry, Judith Serré, 59

Howard, A., 68

Howells, John Mead, 1, 7

Hudson River, 36

Huguenots, 17, 25, 59, 66, 69; Carolina history, 52; character, 18, 39, 52; Charlesfort, 11; church affiliation, 25, 26, 66, 69; industries, 17, 27; politics, 20; settlements, 23, 48, 65, 67, 87

Hyde, Earl of Clarendon, 13

Hyde Park Plantation, 49

Indians, Carolina policy, 15; enslavement, 21; Kiawahs, 15; intermarriage with Negroes, 21; name, 76; sites, 21; trade, 20, 51; Westoes, 15; Yemassee, 24

indigo, dye making, 28; history, 15, 27, 31; prosperity, 28
industries, general provision trade, 16, 33; See Cotton, Indigo, Rice
"Infidelity and Enthusiasm", 26
inland waterway, 16
Innocenti, Humberto, 72
introduction, Howells', 7
Ireland, 15
Irish, 15, 18; Catholics, 18
Irishtown Plantation, 71
Izard family, 29, 79, 81
Izard, Henry, 79
Izard, Patience W. B., 81
Izard, Ralph, p. 50, 79; (with wife) portrait by Copley, 79

Jamestown, 23, 69
"Janet Berkeley", 77
Jehossee Island, 41
Jenkins family, 55
Jervey, Mr. and Mrs. Charles Heyward, 76
Jews, Sephardic, 18
John's Island, 30, 58
Johnson, Fort, 77
Johnson, Governor Sir Nathaniel, 27, 51, 67
Johnston, Frances Benjamin, 5, 7, 9, 89
Jones, Inigo, 61

Kiawah Indians, 15
Kittredge, Benjamine R., 82
kings, 11, 13, 17
Kittery, 87

Lafayette, niece, 72
land allotment, 13
landgraves, Bellinger, 81; Smith, 47, 48; title, 14
Languedoc, 65
Lapham, Samuel, Jr., 1, 7
LAUNCH, THE, house, 40, 83; columns, 46; illustrations, 228; piazzas, 46
Laurens, Henry, 29, 38
Laurens, John, 29
law, Church Establishment, 20; early building, 23; Fundamental Constitution, 13; Indian policy, 21; religious freedom, 26
Lawson, John, 23
LAWSON'S POND, 45, 72, 80, 81; gouge work, 81; illustration, 223
Lee, General Robert E., 78
Lee, Light Horse Harry, 71
Legendre, Gertrude Sanford, 48
Legendre, Sidney, 48
Legendre, Mrs. Sidney J., 48
legends, Fenwick, 57
Le Jau, Dr. Francis, 50
LeNotre, 65
Lewis, Sarah, 69
Lewis, Sedgwick, 69
LEWISFIELD, 27, 44, 46, 69, 70; illustration, 190; piazza, 70
Limerick, 44, 49
Linnaeus, 71
Little Landing, 69
livestock raising, 86
Locke Constitution, See Fundamental Constitution
Locke, John, 13
Lodge, The, 76
log cabins, 23, 58

Long Islanders, 18
Lords Proprietors, 13, 14, 19, 21, 22, 24, 27
Louis XIII, 55
Louis XIV, 17
Louisiana, 21, 38
LOWNDES' GROVE, 46, 74; illustration, 202; portico, 46
Lowndes, William, 74
Loyal Jamaica, 18, 58
Loyalists, 38; expatriation, 37
Lubschez, Ben Judah, 7, 9, 89
Lucas, Dr. Charles, 81
Lucas, Eliza, 28, 56
Lucas family, 81
Lucas, Governor of Antigua, 28
Lucas, Jonathan, 33, 34, 81
Lucas, William, 81
Lynch family, 59

Macauley, historian, 23
Madagascar, 22
Madeira, wine trade, 22
MAGNOLIA GARDENS, 61, 85; illustration, 233
Maine, 18, 87
Maison Carrée, 76
malaria, 34, 69; localities, 35
Manigault, Gabriel, 67; son's education, 29
Manigault family, 41
Manning, John L., 40
Marchmont, Earl of, 33
Marion, General Francis, 65, 70
Marion, Rebecca, 81
marl, 17, 39, 66; building material, 23; The Rocks, 39; Santee, 23
marriages, significance, 25, 28
MARSHLANDS, 77; gouge work, 45, 80; illustrations, 211-214
Martinique, 27
Massachusetts, 18, 77
Maubourg, Elenore Marie Florimonde de Fay la Tour, 72
McRae family, 86
MEDWAY, 23, 24, 44, 47, 48, 53, 82; illustrations, 90-93, plan 48
Medway River, 47
Mestees, Mestizos, 21
Mexico Plantation, 77
Middle Country, 38, 39
MIDDLEBURG, 24, 44, 48, 53, 62, 69; illustrations, 94-96; oldest wooden house, 24, 48; piazza, 46; plan, 48
Middleton, Arthur, 56, 64, 71
Middleton, Edward, 56
Middleton family, English estate, 56
Middleton, Henry, 28, 57, 64, 83
Middleton, John, 57, 73
Middleton, Mary Williams, 64
Middleton, Oliver Hering, 83
MIDDLETON PLACE, 57, 61, 64, 65; garden, 7, 28, 65; illustrations, 174-179
Middleton, Thomas, 57
Middleton, William, 29, 56, 57, 64
Middleton, Williams, 65
Mikell, I. Jenkins, 40, 41
Milford Plantation, 39
Millford Plantation, 40
Millwood Plantation, 40
missions and missionaries, Society for Propagation of Gospel, 26, 50; Spanish, 11
Monck's Corner, 66
Monk, George, 13

Monserrat, 27
Morawetz, Mr. and Mrs. Victor, 59
Morris, Anne Barnett Elliott, 76
Morris, Col. Lewis, 76
Morris, George Washington, 76, 83
Motte, Elizabeth, 59
Motte family, 56
Motte, Frances, 59, 73
Motte, Jacob, 59
Motte, Rebecca Brewton, 59, 73
Moultrie, General William, 30, 39
Mount Desert, 36
MOUNT HOPE, 45, 76, 83; plan, 76; polygonal rooms,
    76
Mount Pleasant, 18
MULBERRY, 24, 27, 51, 52, 53, 54; device, 27, 52;
    illustrations, 106-111; plan, 51; portico, 44, 46

Neck, Charleston, 74
Negroes, admixture with Indians, 21; church communi-
    cants, 67, 84; Federal beneficiaries, 42, 71; Federal
    troops, 61; Gaillard records, 75; "Gippy", 86; importa-
    tion, 15, 16; malaria immunity, 34; "Old Hark", 77;
    relative number, 32; "street", 86; war toll, 30; See
    Slavery
New Amsterdam, 18
New England, 22, 36
New York, 36
Newe, Thomas, 23
Newman, George, 65
Newport, 36
Nîmes, 77
Nisbett family, 82
nobility in Carolina, British, 25, 29; provincial, 14
North Carolina, 19, 41; legal separation, 24; migration,
    32; resorts, 36
NORTH CHACHAN, 65, 66; columns, 46; illustrations,
    180
North Hampton Plantation, 30, 39

Oak Island, 40, 78
OAKLAND, 62; illustrations, 166-168
Oaks, The, 56, 57
Old Exchange Building, 85
"Old Hark", 77
Old Town, 23
oldest houses, brick, 23, 47, 48; wood, 24, 47
Oldfield Plantation, 68
OPHIR, 45, 75, 77, 78, 81; illustration, 221
Orange Quarter, 26
OTRANTO, 71, 76; illustration, 190
Otranto Club, 71; porch, 76

paired doors, 45
Palladian, style, 61, 69
Palladio, 40
Palmer, Joseph, 80
parishes, Christ Church, 53, 62; divisions, 63; establish-
    ment, 20; Goose Creek, 28, 50; Prince William's, 63;
    St. Andrew's, 49; St. Denis, 26, 67; St. Helena's, 63;
    St. James', 69; St. John's, 54, 66, 75, 76, 77; St.
    Stephen's, 28, 31, 37, 67; St. Thomas, 26, 67
Parnassus Plantation, 48, 67; brick 48
Peachtree Plantation, 59
Pendleton, 36
Pennsylvania, 32
peoples, admixture, 25
periods, Colonial, 47-70; Provincial, 47-70, Republican,
    71-87
Peru, 77

Peter's Point, 40, 78
Pettiaugers, 15, 16
Philadelphia, 30, 85
Philip II, 11
photographers, 5, 7, 9, 89
piazzas and columns, 40, 45, 46, 48, 56, 63, 70, 77, 81, 86
Piedmont, 36
Pinckney, Charles Cotesworth, 28
Pinckney, Chief Justice Charles, 29, 59
Pinckney, Eliza Lucas, 28, 56, 60
Pinckney, Elizabeth Motte, 59
Pinckney family, 59; homes, 73
Pinckney, Frances Motte, 59, 73
Pinckney, Harriott, 59
Pinckney, Josephine, 73
Pinckney, Thomas, 28, 59, 73, 74, 76
Pinckney, Thomas II, 59
Pinckney, Captain Thomas, 59
pinelands, 35
Pineville, races, 77; resort, 35
Pinopolis, 30, 35; Baptist settlement, 18
pirates, 22, 58
Place des Vosges, 55
plans, house, Charleston, double and single, 44; pre-rev-
    olutionary repetition, 44; St. John's, 45
plantation houses (not featured), 27, 30, 39, 40, 43, 44,
    45, 48, 56, 59, 63, 65, 67, 68, 69, 71, 73, 77, 78
plantation system, development, 11, 14, 16, 17, 21, 24,
    41; disruption, 37; early houses, 23; effects, cotton, 38;
    origin, 11, 12; Revolution, 31
Plantersville, 35
Plauen, Saxony, 85
pluff mud, 32
Pogson, Henrietta Wragg, 75
Pogson, Rev. Milward, 75, 76
politics, 19, 29; Boone's, 85; Church, 19, 20; Indian
    irritation, 21; planters', 29, 41; 1812 war, 74
polygonal rooms, 45, 76, 79, 83
POMPION HILL CHAPEL, 45, 48, 67, 68; illustra-
    tions, 181-185; plan, 67
Pon Pon, 54, 76, 83, 87
Ponce de Léon, 11
Pondichery, 27
Pope, Dr. and Mrs. Jenkins Mikell, 84
Porcher, Charles Cordes, 81
Porcher, Elizabeth Lydia, 81
Porcher, Frederick Adolphus, 84
Porcher, Peter, 77
Porcher, Philip, 68
Porcher, Col. Thomas, 77, 81
Porcher, Thomas II, 81
Port Royal, 11, 15, 18, 41, 78
Portland stone, 23, 46
Prause, Mr. and Mrs. Walter K., 74
PRESBYTERIAN CHURCH, EDISTO, 37, 40, 84;
    communicants, 26; illustrations, 229-230; plan, 84
Prevost, General, 30
primogeniture law, 32, 36
PRINCE WILLIAM'S CHURCH, SHELDON, 37, 46,
    63; illustrations, 170-173; plan, 63
Prince William's Parish, 63
PROSPECT HILL, 87; illustrations, 237
Protestants, 14

Quakers, 18
Queen Anne's War, 20, 51
Quinby Barony, 67

races, Pineville, 77

Ramsay, historian, 23
Ravenel family, 84
Rebellion Roads, 18
"Red Sea Men", 19, 57
religion, Antipaedobaptists, 18; Covenanters, 18; Dissenters, 17, 18; Dorchester settlement, 18; end of persecution, 20; Establishment, 20, 26; freedom of worship, 18; Huguenots, 17, 18; Irish Catholics, 18; Jews, 18; political row, 19; Quakers, 18; revival in 1800's, 84
Republic, changes, 25, 31
resorts, 35, 36
Restoration, The, 12, 13, 14
restorations, 48, 51, 52, 53, 59, 72, 79, 82, 83, 86
Revolution, American, 27, 29, 31, 36
Revolution of 1719, 24, 27
rice, 11, 20, 21, 22, 32, 42, 73, 77, 82; Lucas' mill, 33, 34, 81; present planting, 86
Richardson, Governor, 40
Rochefoucauld-Liancourt, Duc de la, 61
ROCKS, THE, 37, 39, 43, 45, 75, 78; illustrations, 203-204
Rogers, Mr. and Mrs. James S., 86
roof, gambril (jerkin-headed), 51
Roosevelt, Mr. and Mrs. Nicholas G., 86
Rose Hill Plantation, 73
Rose, Thomas, 49
Royal Government, 24, 55
Russell, Nathaniel, 76
Rutledge, Archibald, 60
Rutledge, Frederick, 72
Rutledge, Frederick II, 72
Rutledge, Harriott Horry, 71

Sage, Mrs. Henry Manning, 43
ST. ANDREW'S CHURCH, 27, 49; illustrations, 97-99
St. Augustine, 11, 12, 15, 16, 27
St. Denis' Parish, 26
St. Giles, Barony of, 14
St. Helena, 12
St. Helena's Sound, 40
ST. JAMES', GOOSE CREEK, 27, 30, 45, 50, 51, 76; earliest Anglican Church, 50; establishment of Church of England, 51; illustrations, 100-105; plan, 50
ST. JAMES', SANTEE, 46, 68, 69; illustrations, 188-189
St. John's, Berkeley, 13, 25, 45, 46, 52, 54, 66, 76, 80, 77, 84, 87; architecture, 45, 46, 75, 76, 77, 81; church, 66; cotton prosperity, 39; devastation, 30; Huguenots, 25, 52; plantations, 52, 75, 76, 77, 80, 81, 84, 87
St. Mary's River, 16
St. Michael's Church, 67; architecture, 45, 48, 67
St. Paul's Church, 37
ST. STEPHEN'S CHURCH, 39, 68, 69; architecture, 45; decline, 37; illustrations, 186-187; indigo site, 28, 31, 39
St. Thomas' Parish, 26
Sams, family, 73; house, tabby, 45, 73
San Marco Castle, 12
Santee-Cooper Project, 53, 77, 78, 81, 87
Santee River, 16; Delta, 33, 59; rice prosperity, 39; settlements, 59, 68, 69, 72, 73, 81
Savannah River, 24
Saxony, 85
Scamozzi, 40
Scotch-Irish, 23, 24, 32
Scotland, 33
Screven, Rev. William, 84, 87
Sea Islands, 12, 16, 28, 30, 41, 62, 84; cotton prosperity, 37, 39, 78; homes, 54, 62, 78 (summer), 35

Seabrook family, 62
SEABROOK'S (TOM) HOUSE, 46, 62; illustrations, 169
SEABROOK'S (WILLIAM) HOUSE, 40, 41, 45, 78, 79; illustrations, 215-216; plan, 78
Sedgwick, Ellery, 77
Serré, Judith, 59
Serré, Noë, 59, 60
Sewee, Bay, 19
Shaftesbury, Earl of, 52; (see also Ashley-Cooper)
Sheldon, Bull estates, 63; See Prince William's Church
Sherman, General, 40, 61, 63, 79
Shonnard, Horatio G., 72
Shonnard, Sophie Meldrim, 72
Shubrick, Col. Thomas, 74
Shurtleff, H. R., 5
Silk Hope, 27, 51, 67
Simms, Mr. and Mrs. Albert Gallatin, 74
Simons, Albert, 1, 7
Simons, Benjamin, 23, 48, 49
Simons, Harriet Porcher, 9
Simons, Keating, 69, 70
Simons, Sarah Lewis, 69
single house, 44, 48
Sinkler family, 76
Sinkler, William, 76
slaves and slavery, Indians, 21; land allotments, 13; Negro, 16, 31, 32, 38, 42; war toll, 21, 30
Smith, Alice R. Huger, 5
Smith, D. E. Huger, 5
Smith, H. A. M., 44
Smith, Mr. and Mrs. J. J. Pringle, 65
Smith, Thomas, 47
Society for the Propagation of the Gospel, missions and missionaries, 26, 50
SOMERSET, 18, 46, 84, 87; illustration, 223; piazza, 46
Somersetshire, 87
SOMERTON, 18, 84-85, 87; columns, 46, 85; illustrations, 231-232
South Carolina Historical and Genealogical Society, 44
Spain and Spanish, 11, 12, 15, 18, 19, 20, 24, 70
SPRINGFIELD, 45, 72, 75, 80, 81; gouge work, 45, 80; illustrations, 218-219; plan, 80
Stone, Mr. and Mrs. Thomas A., 86
Stoney, Augustine, 7
Stoney, Louisa Cheves, 48
Stoney, Mrs. P. G., 48
Stoney, Peter Gaillard, 47, 48
Stoney, Samuel Gaillard, 1, 7
Stoney, Samuel Gaillard (late), 47
Stono River, 58
Storm, Mrs. A. F., 71
STRAWBERRY CHAPEL, 54; illustration, 116
Stuartstown, 18
studs, plantation, 30, 58, 77
Suffolk, 57
Sullivan's Island, 30
summer homes, 34, 35, 69
Summerton, 35
Summerville, 35
Surinam, 18
Swiss, 24
Switzerland, 29

T (Tee), Cooper River, 62, 82
tabby, 12, 45, 73
Thomas, Reverend Samuel, 50
Thomason, C. Y., 87
Thurber, John, 22
Tide Water region, 39
TOMOTLEY, 80-81; illustration, 220

Tomotley Savannah, 81
topography, 16
trade, 16, 22. See Cotton, General Provisions, Indigo, Rice
"The Treasure of Peyre Gaillard", 48
Tuckahoe Plantation, 56
Tuomey, geologist, 23

Up Country, 3, 31

Van Arrsens, Jan, 18, 23, 24, 47
Versailles, Court of, 29
Villepontoux, Francis, 68
Villepontoux, Zachariah, 48, 67, 68
Virginia, 12, 19, 29, 32, 35, 38, 74
Virginia Springs, 36

Wadboo Barony, 31, 65, 66
Wadboo Creek, 23
Walker, carpenter, 75
Wallin, Hendrick, 72
Walnut Grove, 45
Wambaw Creek, 59, 69; church, 69
Wambaw Lodge of Freemasons, 68
WAPPAOOLA, 75; illustrations, 205-206; plan, 76
War of 1812, 27
Waring, J. Waties, 5
wars, see Confederate, French-Indian, French and English,
    Revolution, Revolt of 1719, 1812, World
Warwickshire, 63
Washington, President, 60
Watson, David J., 53
Webber, Mabel L., 44
WEDGE, THE, 81-82; illustrations, 224-225; polygonal
    rooms, 45

Weirnhoudt, Seigneur de, 47
Welsh, 15
West Indians, colonists, 13, 14, 15, 16, 17, 19; Carolina
    aristocracy, 25
West Indies, architecture, 45, 48, 70; slavery, 30, 38
West Virginia Pulp and Paper Co., 57, 62
WHITE HALL, 80, 81; gouge work, 80; illustrations,
    221-222
White House architect, 78
White, John Sims, 86
White, Mrs. John St. Clair, 53
White Point, Cooper River, 62; Charleston, 15, 23
Whitelaw, Robert N. S., 5
Whitfield, George, 26
Whitney gin, 38, 81
Williams, John, 64
Williams, Mary, 64
Williamsburg, 23
Wilton, 76
Winston, Owen, 76, 83
Winyah Bay, 43
Witherspoon family, 23
Woodlawn, 43
Woodward, Mr. and Mrs. Charles H., 82
World Wars, 42, 43
Wragg, Henrietta, 75
Wren, Sir Christopher, 23, 45

Yemassee Indians, 24; territory, 81; war, 23, 24, 27, 51,
    63, 64
Yeshoe, 71
York, Duke of, 18

BIBLIOGRAPHY

Archdale, J.: *A New Description of that Fertile and Pleasant Province of Carolina.* . . . London, 1707. Charleston: A E. Miller, 1822.

Ball, William Watts: *The State that Forgot.* Indianapolis: Bobbs Merrill Company, 1932.

Brown, Louise Fargo: *The First Earl of Shaftesbury.* New York: D. Appleton-Century Company, 1933.

Courtney, W. A. (editor): *The Genesis of South Carolina 1562-1670.* Columbia: The State Company, 1907.

Crane, V. W.: *The Southern Frontier 1670-1732.* Durham: Duke University Press, 1928.

Dalcho, Frederick: *An Historical Account of the Protestant Episcopal Church in South Carolina.* Charleston: A. E. Miller, 1820.

Drayton, J.: *A View of South Carolina.* . . . Charleston: W. P. Young, 1802.

Dubose, Samuel, and Porcher, Frederick A.: *A Contribution to the History of the Huguenots of South Carolina.* New York: The Knickerbocker Press, 1887.

Elzas, Barnett A.: *The Jews of South Carolina.* Philadelphia: J. B. Lippincott Company, 1905.

Gaillard, Thomas: *The History of the Huguenots of South Carolina and their Descendants.* Manuscript.

Harrison, Fairfax: *The John's Island Stud 1750-1788.* Richmond, 1931.

Hewat, A.: *An Historical Account of the Rise and Progress of the Colonies of South Carolina and Georgia.* London: Alexander Donaldson, 1779.

Heyward, Duncan Clinch: *Seed from Madagascar.* Chapel Hill: University of North Carolina Press, 1937.

Hirsch, Arthur Henry: *The Huguenots of Colonial South Carolina.* Durham: Duke University Press, 1928.

Howe, George: *History of the Presbyterian Church in South Carolina.* Columbia: Duffie and Chapman, 1870.

Hutson, Francis Marion, and Todd, John R.: *Prince William's Parish and Plantations.* Richmond: Garrett & Massie, 1935.

Irving, John B.: *A Day on Cooper River.* Second edition, enlarged and edited by Louisa Cheves Stoney. Columbia: The R. L. Bryan Company, 1932.

Kimball, Fiske: *Domestic Architecture of the American Colonies and of the Early Republic.* New York: Charles Scribner's Sons, 1922.

Lawson, John: *A New Voyage to Carolina.* London, 1709.

McCrady, Edward: *History of South Carolina.* Vol. I: *Proprietary Government, 1670-1719;* Vol. II: *Royal Government, 1719-1776;* Vol. III: *Revolution, 1775-1780;* Vol. IV: *Revolution, 1780-1783.* New York: The Macmillan Company, 1897-1902.

Mills, Robert: *Statistics of South Carolina.* Charleston: Hurlbut and Lloyd, 1826.

Olmsted, F. L.: *A Journey in the Seaboard Slave States.* New York: Dix and Edwards, 1856.

Phillips, Ulrich Bonnell: *American Negro Slavery.* New York and London: D. Appleton and Company, 1929.

Phillips, Ulrich Bonnell: *Life and Labor in the Old South.* Boston: Little, Brown and Company, 1929.

Phillips, Ulrich Bonnell (editor): *Plantation and Frontier Documents, 1649-1863.* Cleveland: The Arthur H. Clark Company, 1909.

Pinckney, C. C.: *Life of General Thomas Pinckney.* Boston: Houghton Mifflin & Co., 1895.

Poyas, Mrs.: *The Olden Time of Carolina, by the Octogenarian Lady of Charleston, S. C.* Charleston: S. G. Courtenay & Co., 1855.

Ramsay, David: *The History of South Carolina from the First Settlement in 1670 to the Year 1808.* Vol. II. Charleston: David Longworth, for the author, 1809. Two vols.

Ramsey, Stanley: *Small Houses of the Late Georgian Period, 1750-1820.* Vol. I. London: Technical Journals Ltd., 1919; Vol. II (with J. D. M. Harvey), London: The Architectural Press, 1923. New York: W. Helburn, 1919-23, two vols.

Ravenel, Henry Edmund: *Ravenel Records.* Atlanta: The Franklin Printing and Publishing Company, 1898.

Ravenel, H. H.: *Eliza Pinckney.* New York: Charles Scribner's Sons, 1896.

Ravenel, Mrs. St. Julien: *Charleston: the Place and the People.* New York: The Macmillan Company, 1906.

Rivers, W. J.: *A Chapter in the Early History of South Carolina.* Charleston: Walker, Evans & Cogswell, 1874.

Rivers, W. J.: *Sketch of the History of South Carolina to the Close of the Proprietary Government by the Revolution of 1719.* Charleston: McCarter & Co., 1856.

Salley, A. S., Jr. (editor): *Narratives of Early Carolina 1650-1708.* New York: Charles Scribner's Sons, 1911. In *Original Narratives of Early American History.*

Sanderson, J., *et al.: Biography of the Signers to the Declaration of Independence.* Philadelphia: J. M. Sanderson, 1820-27.

Simons, Albert, and Lapham, Samuel: *Charleston, South Carolina.* Vol. I of *Octagon Library of Early American Architecture.* New York: American Institute of Architects, 1927.

Small, Tunstall, and Woodbridge, Christopher: *Houses of the Wren and Early Georgian Periods.* London: The Architectural Press, 1928.

Smith, Alice R. Huger, and Smith, D. E. Huger: *The Dwelling Houses of Charleston, South Carolina.* Philadelphia and London: J. B. Lippincott Company, 1917.

Smith, H. A. M.: *The Baronies of South Carolina.* Charleston: South Carolina Historical Society, 1931.

Thomas, Ebenezer Smith: *Reminiscences of the Last Sixty-five Years.* . . . Hartford: Case, Tiffany & Burnham, 1840.

Wallace, D. D.: *The History of South Carolina.* New York: American Historical Society, 1934.

Ware, William Rotch (editor): *The Georgian Period.* . . . Boston: American Architect and Building News Company, 1901; New York: The American Architect, 1908.

Webber, Mabel L. (editor): *The South Carolina Historical and Genealogical Magazine.*

Woolson, C. F.: *Up the Ashley and Cooper.* In *Harper's Magazine,* Vol. 52, December, 1875.

A Letter from South Carolina: written (1710) by a Swiss Gentleman to his Friend at Bern. Second edition. London: printed for J. Clarke, 1732.

Historical Collections of South Carolina. . . . Compiled . . . by B. R. Carroll. Vol. I. New York: Harper and Brothers, 1836. Two vols.

Plantation Book of Peter Gaillard of the Rocks, St. John's, Berkeley.

Plantation Book of Joseph Palmer of Springfield, St. John's, Berkeley.

Records of Mesne Conveyance, Office of Recorder, Charleston, South Carolina.

The Shaftesbury Papers and Other Records relating to Carolina and the First Settlement on Ashley River prior to . . . 1676. . . . Edited by Langdon Cheves. South Carolina Historical Society Collections, 1857-59, Vol. V.

The Works in Architecture of Robert and James Adam, Esquires. Cleveland: J. H. Jensen, 1916 (reprint of copy in Avery Library, Columbia University). Original edition published in London, 1773-1822.

Vestry Book of Christ Church Parish.

Vestry Book of St. Stephen's Parish.

Will Books, Office of Probate Court, Charleston, South Carolina.

FIFTEEN HUNDRED COPIES OF THIS FIFTH EDI-TION HAVE BEEN PRINTED ON ORDER OF THE EXECUTIVE BOARD OF THE CAROLINA ART AS-SOCIATION BY THE PRESS OF THE R. L. BRYAN COMPANY, COLUMBIA, S. C. ❧ SET IN CASLON OLD FACE ❧ PRINTED ON WARREN'S LUSTRO GLOSS ENAMEL, SUBSTANCE NO. 100 ❧ ENGRAV-INGS AND PLATES BY STANDARD ENGRAVING COMPANY, INC., WASHINGTON, D. C., AND CARO-LINA ENGRAVING COMPANY, COLUMBIA, S. C.

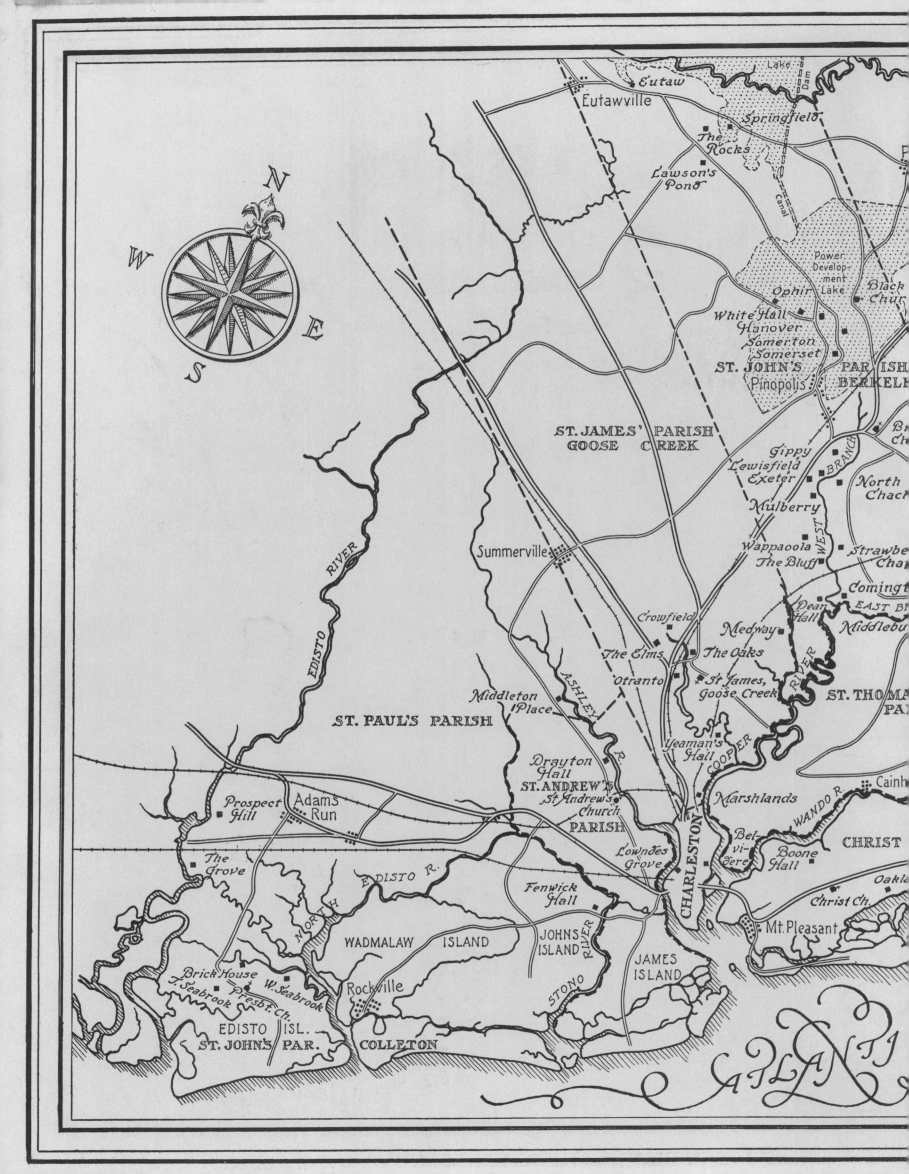